UConn
35-0

The Championship Season of the 1994-95 Women's Basketball Team

• Published by

The Hartford Courant

• Printed by

Times Mirror Higher Education Group
Dubuque, Iowa

• Both owned by

The Times Mirror Company

On the cover:
Rebecca Lobo lets the crowd at Gampel Pavilion know where
she and her team stand after returning from Minneapolis.

RICHARD MESSINA PHOTO

Above:
Jennifer Rizzotti, right, and Rebecca Lobo enjoy the moment
after beating Tennessee to take hold of the national championship.

BRAD CLIFT PHOTO

On the back cover:
Geno Auriemma has cut down all the obstacles in his team's way
and can enjoy the national championship.

BRAD CLIFT PHOTO

BOOK STAFF

GREG GARBER
BRUCE BERLET
Writers

PAULA BRONSTEIN
BRAD CLIFT
ALBERT DICKSON
JOHN DUNN
RICK HARTFORD
MICHAEL KODAS
MICHAEL McANDREWS
RICHARD MESSINA
SHANA SURECK-MEI
SHERRY PETERS
Photographers

MARK LEARY
Editor

JOHN SCANLAN
Picture Editor

RANDY COX
Art Director
Design Consulting
Albuquerque, New Mexico

KATHY WROBEL
Assistant Editor

CHERYL MAGAZINE
Courant Assistant Managing Editor
Photography & Graphics

KAREN LAVALLEE
Color printer

DENNIS YONAN
DAN CORJULO
VICTOR DURAO
DAVID KOOI
Courant photo lab technicians

JAY SPIEGEL
PAUL ROSANO
Proofreaders

ROBERT J. URILLO
Courant Commercial
Printing Manager

SUSAN ACKER
DENNIS SCHAIN
SHARON MULLIGAN
KAREN SUSSLER
LIEVANNA GORE
ANN EICKER
STACEY HURLEY
Marketing

THE COURANT

MICHAEL E. WALLER
Publisher

DAVID S. BARRETT
Editor

MARTY PETTY
Senior Vice President
& General Manager

LOUIS J. GOLDEN
Vice President/Marketing
& Business Development

CLIFFORD L. TEUTSCH
Managing Editor

G. CLAUDE ALBERT
PAM LUECKE
Deputy Managing Editors

JEFF OTTERBEIN
Sports Editor

THOMAS F. McGUIRE
Picture Editor

• Copyright © 1995
by *The Hartford Courant*

• Published in April, 1995 by
The Hartford Courant
285 Broad Street
Hartford, Connecticut 06115

• All rights reserved. No part of this
book may be reproduced without the
written permission of the publisher.

• *Library of Congress*
Catalog Card Number 95-76791

• *ISBN 0-9646638-0-5*

• *Profits benefit Hartford's*
Camp Courant and the
University of Connecticut

• *This book is printed on 80 lb. Consoweb*
Brilliant Gloss by the Times Mirror Higher
Education Group, Dubuque, Iowa.
This book was typeset using the New
Caledonia, Helvetica Inserat, Helvetica
Condensed and Zapf Dingbat text families.
The cover is UV-coated and printed on
120 lb. Carolina Cover stock.

At right, as the team gathers on
the court after stopping the Vols,
Rebecca Lobo, as she has done so
often, reaches out to her teammates.

BRAD CLIFT PHOTO

Simply the best

For 128 days, they were perfect: 35 victories in 35 games.

And then, the day after the University of Connecticut women's basketball team won the national championship, the state still could not take its eyes off the Huskies.

They were still in the air, on a flight home from Minneapolis, when the local television stations gathered at Bradley International Airport to begin more than three hours of live coverage. The Huskies stepped off the plane and were greeted by more than 1,500 fans. There were roses from the governor, more interviews and congratulations.

By the time the team arrived in Storrs,

more than 8,000 fans had been drawn into Gampel Pavilion. They thanked the team for an uplifting season. And then the Huskies thanked them.

"We think we have something special here," said Rebecca Lobo, UConn's most eloquent player, on and off the court. "In a way, it has nothing to do with the basketball court. It has to do with how we feel about each other, and you."

They never seemed worried about the score or who they were playing.

All they wanted to do was get on the court and have fun.

From left, Kara Wolters, Meghan Pattyson, Tonya Cardoza, Nykesha Sales, Jennifer Rizzotti (back), Geno Auriemma, Jill Gelfenbien, Rebecca Lobo, Missy Rose, Pam Webber and Kelley Hunt face their fans once more while being honored at a pep rally at Gampel Pavilion.

RICK HARTFORD PHOTO

This is a call
Geno Auriemma
agrees with as he talks
to President Clinton.
It was the first time
a president called
a women's champion.
Auriemma's daughter,
Alysa, is in
the background.

The Huskies mascot finds
time to baby a young
audience member
at a rally at Gampel
Pavilion to honor
the women.

PAULA BRONSTEIN
AND
RICHARD MESSINA
PHOTOS

Though they seldom received the proper respect — weak conference, weak schedule, four home games in the NCAA Tournament, the doubters said — they captured the imagination of those who enjoy watching players dive on the floor to save a ball when leading by 30, 40 and 50 points.

After the victory laps had been taken, the nets snipped and the call from President Clinton completed, it was left to the Huskies' coach to put things in perspective.

Geno Auriemma — who joked his mother, Marsiella, put him on a boat in Montella, Italy, at age 7 and told him to go win a national championship — drove his team to an unprecedented record and unparalleled 33.2-point average margin of victory.

"Good things happen to good people," Auriemma said, "and if you're Rebecca Lobo and Pam Webber — and you're the absolutely best people in the world — then in a fairy-tale world, this is the way it's supposed to end.

"Too many times it doesn't, but this is the way it's supposed to end."

Who could have imagined when the Huskies gathered in mid-August to install a new motion offense before a 12-day trip to Europe, the team's only loss the next 7$^{1/2}$ months would come against a club team from Valenciennes, France?

Jennifer Rizzotti is aware of the link between her team and its fans and lets them know she appreciates their loyalty.

SHERRY PETERS PHOTO

There were some very special moments:

• In her Big East debut against Villanova, freshman Nykesha Sales drives to the basket, puts the ball behind her back, makes a reverse layup and is fouled. It's part of an 80-42 victory and the start of the second unbeaten (18-0) regular season in conference history.

• The play that frames the Huskies' chemistry comes in the Jan. 13 game against 19th-ranked Seton Hall. With an 80-36 victory well in hand, Jennifer Rizzotti dives face-first onto the floor between two defenders and tips the ball to Kim Better, who saves it to Carla Berube, who gets it back to Rizzotti. Moments later, Rizzotti passes it inside to Lobo, who makes a no-look, touch pass to Kara Wolters for a layup.

• Three days later, with Lobo in foul trouble and her broken pinky covered with tape, the Huskies climb to the top of women's basketball with a

More than 8,000 fans cheer their conquering heroes as an imported score, via Minneapolis and the national championship game, flashes on the Gampel Pavilion scoreboard.

RICK HARTFORD PHOTO

77-66 victory over three-time national champion Tennessee. A couple years earlier, people wouldn't come to Gampel Pavilion, but this day they wouldn't leave, saluting the Huskies for nearly a half-hour after the game.

• Senior Night produces a flood of memories and tears, as Lobo, Webber and walk-on Jill Gelfenbien play their final regular season game at home. The St. John's players and coaches stand when Lobo is introduced and walks onto the court with her father, Dennis, and mother, RuthAnn, whose cancer is in remission. The Huskies win 103-56 to complete their second consecutive unbeaten season at home.

With an 85-49 victory over Seton Hall and a second consecutive Big East tournament title safely in hand, Rizzotti dives for a loose ball and the Pirates' Tahnee Heins falls on Rizzotti's arm. Rizzotti suffers a hyperextended right elbow, but is in the starting lineup when the

It's a moment Kim Better wants to capture:
Kara Wolters and the Huskies mascot decide the situation calls for a few steps.

RICHARD MESSINA PHOTO

UConn President Harry Hartley is pleased with where Kara Wolters and the women's team sit: at the top of women's basketball.

RICHARD MESSINA PHOTO

Huskies begin their seventh consecutive NCAA Tournament appearance with a 105-75 victory over Maine.

• UConn trails for the first time at halftime in the East Regional final against Virginia, then rallies for a 67-63 victory. In the final minute, Wolters blocks a shot. Jamelle Elliott implores her teammates to make one final defensive stop, which results in a five-second violation on an inbounds play. Lobo then makes an emphatic block of Wendy Palmer's three-point shot.

The Huskies are headed to the Final Four for the second time.

• Though All-Americans Lobo, Rizzotti and Wolters are in foul trouble most of the first half, UConn rallies from its second halftime deficit of the season to beat Tennessee 70-64 and win the school's first national title in basketball.

With 1 minute, 51 seconds left and the score 61-61, Rizzotti takes a long rebound and sprints the length of the court. Tennessee's Michelle Marciniak is the only one between Rizzotti and the

basket. She spins Marciniak with a cross-over dribble and lays the ball in left-handed. UConn never loses the lead.

When the game ends, the UConn band plays "We Are the Champions" and "Respect." Auriemma hugs every player, his staff and his family before cutting down the final strand of net. He is carried by his players to the locker room, and an hour later he takes a call from the White House, a first for a women's basketball champion.

The spoils of victory are immense:

Southwick, Mass., Lobo's hometown, renames the half-mile entrance road to the regional high school Rebecca Lobo Way. A selectman says Lobo, an honor student coming off a straight-A first semester, has shown the way to get ahead in education.

For the third time in history, Sports Illustrated produces a cover for a regional audience. New England gets Rizzotti dashing after a ball, while the rest of the country gets the men's NCAA championship game.

Lobo holds her own with CBS's David Letterman in a five-minute interview.

Letterman: "Your coach is a man, isn't he?

What is that like? Is that legal?"

Lobo: "He's not bad looking, so we don't mind."

What will they do for an encore?

With a recruiting class rated the second-best in the nation — Tammy Arnold, Amy Duran, Amy Hughes, Courtney Gaine and transfer Sarah Northway — the Huskies' future seems secure.

• Arnold, a 6-foot-3 center, is rated the No. 1 post player in the country on the No. 1 team, Oregon City in Oregon, and could be the heir apparent to Lobo.

• Duran, a 6-foot swing player from Bethesda, Md., is a second-team All-American and rated the 13th-best player in the nation.

• Hughes, a 5-10 guard from Sciotoville, Ohio,

is a third-team All-American who should help give Rizzotti needed rest.

• Gaine (5-10) and Northway (6-1) will give the Huskies more versatility and depth at forward and guard.

"We could have a better team next season because of more quality players, but that doesn't mean we'll be better," Auriemma said. "We had that something special this season that's difficult to recapture.

"We still have — and always will have — special kids, but only the blessed are fortunate to enjoy those very special moments." ■

A quick show of hands at Gampel Pavilion tells you all you need to know about the direction the Huskies have taken.

RICHARD MESSINA PHOTO

"We still have – and always will have – special kids, but only the blessed are fortunate to enjoy those very special moments."

• UConn coach
Geno Auriemma

Pam Webber pauses
while trying to amplify
to the fans at Gampel Pavilion
her thoughts about the past four
years at UConn.

RICHARD MESSINA PHOTO

■ CHAPTER ONE

Where it all began

Nov. 10
UConn 61
Athletes in Action 58

Nov. 16
UConn 100
Rossianka 77

Nov. 26
UConn 107
Morgan State 27

Nov. 27
UConn 92
Rhode Island 59

Dec. 4
UConn 80
Villanova 42

*(Box scores,
Pages 129-130)*

Beginnings are often tentative affairs. A new basketball season means, by definition, a new basketball team. Even though the University of Connecticut women's team returned eight letter-winners from the 1993-94 team that won 30 of 33 games, there was clearly a new feel to this group.

Where and how, for instance, would freshman forward Nykesha Sales, the USA Today National Player of the Year, fit in? Would senior All-American Rebecca Lobo fulfill the vast promise she had shown the year before? Could 6-foot-7 center Kara Wolters, now a sophomore, follow Lobo's convincing lead? Did point guard Jennifer Rizzotti have the intuitive skills to direct UConn to a new level?

In UConn's exhibition opener against Athletes in Action, Huskies junior Kim Better isn't daunted by Kelly Porter. Late in the game, Better, 5 feet 7, got around 6-8 Heidi Gillingham for a rebound.

MICHAEL
MCANDREWS
PHOTO

The most pressing question: How would the team react after its devastating 81-69 NCAA Tournament loss to North Carolina? Remember, UNC earned a trip to the Final Four and an eventual national title by beating UConn. Would the Huskies return with a stronger commitment, or shrink from the challenge?

The first public opportunity to gauge these issues came Nov. 10, when Athletes in Action visited Storrs for an exhibition game. Coach Geno Auriemma, a man with a sense of history and symmetry, chose to start the players who started the team's NCAA Tournament games: Lobo, Wolters, Rizzotti, Jamelle Elliott and Pam Webber.

UConn, a team that was ranked no lower than sixth in the national preseason polls, struggled against a group of former college all-stars before 5,937 at Gampel Pavilion.

With just more than seven minutes left, Lobo left the game with only six points and six rebounds and a bruised left knee. The Huskies, looking rather hopeless, trailed by five at the time.

Somehow, Wolters and Sales each scored six points down the stretch, then junior guard Kim Better made the play of the game. At 5-7, Better out-positioned AIA's 6-8 Heidi

Jennifer Rizzotti, unable to play against Rossianka because of back spasms, sees the beginnings of an exceptional breed of basketball.

PAULA BRONSTEIN PHOTO

Gillingham for a muscular rebound and threw in a shot that gave UConn a two-point lead with 29 seconds left. Sales added a free throw and the Huskies won, 61-58.

Still, the Huskies committed 22 turnovers, 14 in the first half. Auriemma admitted he was disappointed.

Part of the reason UConn passes teams with ease: Jennifer Rizzotti. Far right, Rizzotti is forced out of bounds by Morgan State's Faith McGriff in a 107-27 victory in the season opener. Rizzotti had seven points and six assists in 16 minutes as UConn won by its biggest margin in history.

SHANA SURECK-MEI PHOTOS

"I know I can't be like that," he said. "I expect them to play like they played last March. But you also learn this: we have kids who can step up and win the game."

When the Nov. 16 game against Rossianka of Moscow arrived, the Huskies had had their share of international competition. In August, UConn toured France, Belgium and Italy for two weeks and won four of five games. Unlike the opener, this exhibition never reached a climax.

UConn led 49-39 at the half and won, 100-77. Wolters led UConn with 25 points and Lobo added 19 points and 10 rebounds.

The only moment of drama occurred in pregame warmups when Rizzotti suffered back spasms. She watched the game on crutches.

After the game, Lobo still wasn't satisfied with the Huskies' level of play. "We played a lot better

offensively," she said. "We kind of had to, since our defense gave up so many points. We still have a lot of things to work on in practice."

I t was Morgan State's grave misfortune to be next in line when the games began to officially count. The Huskies were ranked third in the country and had been locked up in Auriemma's torturous practices for 10 days.

The date: Nov. 26. The event: The Hartford Courant Connecticut Classic. The result: a 107-27 victory, technically the biggest blowout in the 20-year, 528-game history of the UConn women's program.

The game's critical mass came early; with the score 6-6, UConn disappeared with a 25-0 run. Even with Auriemma's liberal substitutions, the Huskies produced some epic numbers. They set school records for points and margin of victory, surpassing a 103-45 victory over Colgate in November 1993.

Lobo produced 18 points, 13 rebounds, a career-best seven assists and four blocked shots. She set a UConn record for rebounds, pushing her total to 938.

Auriemma observed that the team had taken another step in gathering a collective confidence. "If we learned anything on our

European trip, it's that we can't concern ourselves with who we play or what we're going to do," he said. "The bottom line in being a successful team is how good you are at doing the things you do and, secondarily, how good you are at preventing someone from doing what they want to do."

Rhode Island, a 78-59 first-round winner over Santa Clara, earned the dubious honor of opposing UConn in the final. The game was tied at 28 with 5 minutes, 33 seconds left in the first half but the Huskies scored the last 14 points of the half.

The final was 92-59 before 5,782 at Gampel and it was a result typical of the looming season. The Huskies felt Rhode Island had been a formidable opponent, yet had won by 33.

UConn, led by Lobo's game-high 21 points, 12 rebounds and seven assists, won its fifth consecutive Classic title.

The Huskies were 2-0 in the regular season, but the question was, how good, really, were they? The Villanova game, the Big East opener Dec. 4, would provide a context. Only one week earlier, Villanova had lost to No. 6 Alabama, 73-57, in a game that had been tied with nine minutes left.

This is the season
the full talents
of Kara Wolters,
far left, were released.
Wolters led UConn
with 15 points
against Villanova.

Into the middle
of UConn's dominance
walked freshman
Nykesha Sales (42),
left, who had 14 points
in 23 minutes
against Rhode Island.

PAULA BRONSTEIN PHOTOS

Scanning the box score after the Villanova game, the casual observer might have seen this line and assumed a UConn loss:

Lobo, 4-for-15 from the field, nine points.

Nevertheless, UConn defeated Villanova 80-42 with a terrific display of balance. Before 6,124 at Gampel, Wolters (15 points), Elliott (13), a healthy Rizzotti (12) and Sales (11) carried UConn's offense. Typically, Lobo anchored the defense with 16 rebounds, five blocked shots and three steals.

After the game, in which UConn held his shooters to 21.9 percent, Villanova coach Harry Perretta had this sobering thought for future opponents:

"UConn is better than I thought. They're better than they were last year because now both Lobo and Wolters score on you inside. They don't lose anything when Lobo goes out." ∎

As Chapter One ends:
UConn is 3-0 and ranked No. 3 in the nation.

Far left: With Kara Wolters, left, and Rebecca Lobo (50), Rhode Island is easily turned away as the Huskies totaled 15 blocks.

Three games and three victories into the season and Rebecca Lobo, left, and UConn are already worth a serious look.

PAULA BRONSTEIN PHOTOS

Nykesha Sales, left, and Rebecca Lobo are two of the more absorbing figures the UConn women's program has produced.

PAULA BRONSTEIN PHOTO

"UConn is better than I thought. They're better than they were last year because now both Lobo and Wolters score on you inside. They don't lose anything when Lobo goes out."

• Villanova coach Harry Perretta

■ CHAPTER TWO

Who can stop them?

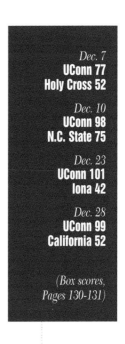

Dec. 7
UConn 77
Holy Cross 52

Dec. 10
UConn 98
N.C. State 75

Dec. 23
UConn 101
Iona 42

Dec. 28
UConn 99
California 52

(Box scores,
Pages 130-131)

here are no tricks in college basketball; videotape has forever removed the element of surprise. So it was only after a few minutes of uncomfortable viewing that Holy Cross coach Bill Gibbons began to understand he had a single, desperate, defensive choice when UConn visited on Dec. 7.

Teams were playing the tall and terrifying Huskies loose out on the perimeter, which allowed Rebecca Lobo the freedom to pass or shoot from the low post. The 1-3 Crusaders used two, sometimes three players on Lobo and forced UConn's other players to shoot over them.

For a while, it worked. Playing in front of a record crowd (2,583) at the Hart Center in Worcester, Holy Cross trailed 34-21 at the half before losing, 77-52.

The Huskies shot a miserable 28-for-78 from the field (35.9 percent), their worst in 40 games. UConn made only 7 of 24 three-pointers. Inside, Lobo (3-for-13, 10 points) and Wolters (1-for-5, four points) did not handle the attention well in their first road game.

"I've never seen a team pack in a zone like that," forward Jamelle Elliott said. "We were a bit out of sync and took more jump shots than we wanted."

It was Elliott (18 points, 12 rebounds) who carried the game to Holy Cross, backed by guard Jennifer Rizzotti (16 points, six steals) and freshman Nykesha Sales (15 points, four steals in 20 minutes).

UConn, now ranked second in the nation behind Tennessee, was 4-0. There were three more nonconference games in December before the Big East schedule began in earnest. The question was, after two consecutive games laced with disappointing shooting, would the Huskies remember how to find the basket?

Kim Better, second from left, helps give UConn grounds for another victory, this time against Bridget Gardner and Holy Cross. Pam Webber, left, is there to help back the play.

SHANA SURECK-MEI PHOTO

The searing answer was delivered Dec. 10, in front of 1,066 witnesses at North Carolina State's Reynolds Coliseum.

"UConn had a perfect second half, offensively," said N.C. State's Tammy Gibson after the Huskies defeated the Wolfpack, 98-75.

Indeed, UConn shot 73.1 percent in that second half and 59.3 for the game in winning its fifth game of the year. The Huskies made 9 of 11 three-point shots and had five players in double figures.

Lobo (24 points), Elliott, who tied a career high with 21 points, and Rizzotti (14 points) were backed by Carla Berube (11) and Sales (10).

As a partial response to the Holy Cross game, coach Geno Auriemma moved Lobo outside, where the 6-foot-4 forward hit a three-pointer and sent UConn on a run of

Celebration becomes a familiar thing for Rebecca Lobo, who reached back for 25 points on 11-for-11 shooting to stop Iona.

JOHN DUNN PHOTO

11 consecutive scoring possessions. Lobo did this despite spraining her right thumb the previous day.

"I felt if we moved Rebecca out on the perimeter she would be a moving target and they'd have a hard time finding her," Auriemma said. "And that's exactly what happened.

"[The media] voted Rebecca preseason player of the year. I don't know if she's the best player in the country, but I definitely think she's the most versatile and had a chance to prove that today."

Lost in the wake of UConn's newfound offense was the convincing nature of the victory. The Huskies' point total was the highest ever allowed by N.C. State at home.

After a 13-day hiatus for final exams and Christmas shopping, the Huskies returned for a Dec. 23 meeting with Iona at Gampel Pavilion. Iona, 7-20 the previous year, was badly outmatched.

The score was 101-42, but Auriemma was moved by the Gaels' effort. Perhaps he saw a little of his first UConn team, the 1985-86

After a rebound, Rebecca Lobo is leaning toward taking a shot, despite the efforts of Holy Cross' Karen Juda, left, and Alison Dietz.

Jennifer Rizzotti, above, lets California's Eliza Sokolowska know that the level of competition is usually heightened in Storrs, while, far right, Carla Berube steps it up a little against Patti Czepiec.

SHANA SURECK-MEI
PHOTOS

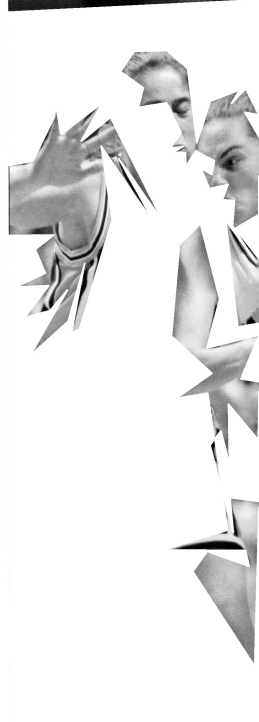

version that finished 12-15. Maybe he was moved by sentiment; the coach's first victory came against Iona. In any case, Auriemma addressed both teams after the game, something he had never done.

"I've been there and I know what [Iona coach Harry Hart] is trying to do," Auriemma said. "So I wish him well.

"I told their kids they're a lot better than the Iona team we played 10 years ago. I said I didn't want them to think losing to the No. 2 team by [59] points means they stink — because they don't. You have to believe in yourself and what you're trying to do."

The 6,725 at Gampel Pavilion weren't privy to Auriemma's poignant address, but they saw UConn hit 100 points for the second time. It was a season's worth of highlights in 40 minutes:

Here was Lobo blocking a shot, then finishing Sales' spin and pass for a layup. There was freshman reserve Kelley Hunt's high-post pass to Sales, who caught it in midair and laid it in. Walk-on Jill Gelfenbien, the soccer team's goalkeeper, scored

her first points on a 6-foot bank shot 5 seconds before halftime.

Ultimately, the Huskies shot a season-high 62.3 percent and scored the second-highest total in their history, approaching the 107 points scored against Morgan State.

Five days later, in a similar game at Gampel, it nearly happened again. Pity California. Some 3,000 miles from home, the Golden Bears quickly were out of the game.

A sellout crowd of 8,241 roared with each basket and with only 8 minutes, 41 seconds elapsed, UConn had 25 points. California had none. It was 88-28 with 9:07 remaining when Auriemma pulled the starters for good. The score was 99-52.

Lobo, who had 11 points in her team's opening run, outscored California 16-13 in the first half and also had 10 rebounds, the second making her the first UConn player to have 1,000 points and 1,000 rebounds. She finished with 18 points and 16 rebounds. Even more encouraging, Wolters had 20 points, nine rebounds and five blocks.

And so, at the close of 1994, UConn was basically perfect. The Huskies' 7-0 record matched the best in school history. And while Connecticut was buzzing about the school's undefeated men's and women's teams, Auriemma and his associate coach, Chris Dailey, were busy tending to the business of feeding a growing dynasty.

Auriemma traveled to Ohio to watch Oregon City (Ore.) and UConn recruit Tammy Arnold, a 6-3 center averaging 23 points, in a high school tournament. Dailey was in Virginia scouting two other recruits, Amy Duran and Courtney Gaine of Bethesda, Md. ■

As Chapter Two ends:
UConn is 7-0 and ranked No. 2.

California's Deb Oldenburger finds that no matter the circumstances, it's tough to tangle with Jennifer Rizzotti.

SHANA SURECK-MEI PHOTO

■ CHAPTER THREE

A *hundred ways to win*

oach Geno Auriemma arrived at Storrs in 1985 with very little to lose. It is hard, after all, to fall below the floor.

It was Auriemma's first college head coach job and, at the same time, the UConn women's basketball team had had only a single winning season in its 11 years.

A decade later, it all seemed so remote. Here was Auriemma, with a record of 199-81, on the threshold of his 200th victory – an average of 20 victories each year – and the season was young.

The opponent Jan. 2 was Pittsburgh, a 7-2 team that had placed third in the 1994 National Women's Invitational Tournament. It was fitting that Auriemma's 200th victory provided second-ranked UConn (8-0)

Jan. 2
UConn 100
Pittsburgh 67

Jan. 5
UConn 103
Georgetown 64

Jan. 7
UConn 98
St. John's 64

Jan. 11
UConn 104
Providence 50

Jan. 13
UConn 80
Seton Hall 36

(Box scores,
Pages 132-133)

Seniors Pam Webber, right, and Rebecca Lobo have had a part in more than 100 of coach Geno Auriemma's victories.

SHANA SURECK-MEI PHOTO

with its fastest start ever.

The Huskies routed Pittsburgh 100-67 before 7,212 at Gampel Pavilion. In doing so, they extended their home winning streak to 25, including the NCAA Tournament.

Guard Jennifer Rizzotti scored a season-high 22 points and reserve Kim Better a career-high 15 as UConn shot a season-high 63.5 percent.

"It's a great accomplishment, considering he hasn't been coaching that long," said Rebecca

Lobo, who scored five points, one off her career low. (She had four four-point games as a freshman.) "It didn't put any pressure on us, but it did give us a little extra incentive to win it for him."

The team was performing at an unprecedented level. The 40-point blowouts — even on the road as a highly ranked team — were becoming routine. As was the case with Auriemma's 200th victory, the Huskies were learning how to find motivation whenever and wherever it surfaced.

Three nights later at Georgetown's McDonough Arena, UConn took care of business with a typically consistent performance. This time, the motivation came courtesy of Boston

Kelley Hunt, left, and Brenda Marquis are aware coach Geno Auriemma is fond of having the last word.

SHANA SURECK-MEI PHOTO

A concept UConn likes to run by opponents: putting the ball in the hands of Nykesha Sales, who avoids Seton Hall's Rukaiyah Walker.

ALBERT DICKSON
PHOTO

College. The night before, the Eagles had upset 20th-ranked Seton Hall.

"That made us realize that on the road it's going to be a contest," Rizzotti said. "Because everyone's going to be ready to play, especially at home."

The score was UConn 103, Georgetown 64 — the second consecutive game the Huskies (9-0) reached 100 points and the fourth time in nine games. To put that in perspective, consider that UConn had reached 100 only twice in its previous 20 seasons.

Freshman Nykesha Sales and Rizzotti each had a game-high 21 points. Rizzotti scored 10 points in an 18-4 run. UConn had trailed 8-2, its largest deficit of the season. Sophomore forward Carla Berube scored a season-high 13 points, nine in a 16-0 run at the end of the first half. Jamelle Elliott, the junior forward, produced 11 points and 15 rebounds, tying a career high.

Jamelle Elliott gets a pass off through the triangle double team of Seton Hall's Texlin Quinney, left, and Dana Wynne.

ALBERT DICKSON PHOTO

Lobo was again curiously quiet, scoring only nine points. It was the first time in 100 career games that she had failed to reach double figures in back-to-back games.

There was a decided upside to Lobo's brief struggles on offense; it created room for Elliott, Rizzotti and Kara Wolters. And Sales. Coming off the bench, the freshman had been playing significant minutes and scoring regularly. The Georgetown game gave Sales nine consecutive games in double figures, tying the UConn freshman record set by Kris Lamb in 1986. Sales was the only Husky player to score in double figures every game.

On cue, against St. John's Jan. 7, Lobo emerged from the double- and triple-teams that had dogged her the two previous games. Inexplicably, the Red Storm elected to play Lobo straight up and she scored 24 points in a 98-64 victory at Alumni Hall.

Lobo made 8 of 13 shots for the Huskies, who were now 10-0. She added seven rebounds, giving her 581 in 55 Big East games to break the conference record of Georgetown's Leni Wilson. She credited the move from a four-game-old ponytail, back to her trademark braid.

"My shot has been in the icebox," Lobo said, "so I guess this is a coming out. I told someone if the braid didn't work I might try pigtails the next game."

Meanwhile, Sales scored 15 points, setting a team rookie record for consecutive games

A lesson for Providence: Pam Webber can hurt you with the ball or without. She had nine points and a team-high five assists.

RICHARD MESSINA PHOTOS

(10) in double figures.

The game against No. 1 Tennessee was nine days away, but people outside the program were already looking past Providence and Seton Hall.

"We're not thinking about Tennessee because the other two teams are very capable of beating us," Rizzotti said. "Providence has beaten us, and Seton Hall beat us last season, so that gave us a little anger. We'll be fired up."

And they were. Jan. 11, at Gampel Pavilion, the Huskies showed little pity for a team that was down to only five healthy players as the game concluded. UConn beat Providence 104-50, giving the Huskies (11-0) their fifth game at or over 100.

Auriemma spread around the minutes and the reserves responded with terrific games. Berube produced a season-high 18 points; Better, a career-high 17.

It appeared it would be a different matter against Seton Hall. The Pirates (13-2) were ranked 19th in the nation. Seton Hall handed UConn its only Big East loss the year before.

But Jan. 13 at Gampel it wasn't even close. Before 7,659, UConn pressed, then depressed, Seton Hall, winning, 80-36.

Lobo was monstrous. She had 13 points, 14 rebounds and a school-record nine blocks before a dislocated pinky cost her a chance for a triple-double. UConn's oppressive defense — featuring a team-record 17 blocked shots — forced the Pirates into 15-for-75 shooting.

And now, finally, No. 1 would meet No. 2 in three days.

UConn was a lofty 12-0 and the average margin of victory was 42.4 points. Seton Hall's Phyllis Mangina joined the growing number of Big East coaches to back UConn in the anticipated game on national television.

"I think," said Mangina, "we just played against the best team in the country." ■

As Chapter Three ends: UConn is 12-0 and ranked No. 2.

"I think we just played against the best team in the country."

- **Seton Hall coach Phyllis Mangina**

Kerri Chatten, floor, and Sarah Miller (12) of Providence see just what it takes to tackle the job of stopping Rebecca Lobo.

RICHARD MESSINA PHOTO

■ CHAPTER FOUR

The one they wanted

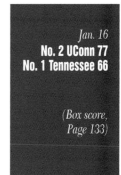

Jan. 16
No. 2 UConn 77
No. 1 Tennessee 66

*(Box score,
Page 133)*

While UConn was ranked anywhere from third to sixth in national preseason polls, there was no doubt who was on top. The University of Tennessee, for which a frightening 10 of 11 letter-winners returned from a 31-2 team, was No. 1 in every poll.

The Lady Volunteers had lost to Louisiana Tech in the NCAA Tournament's round of 16, but they found equilibrium and won their first 16 games in 1994-95. Thus, it was No. 1 vs. No. 2 in a Martin Luther King Day matinee at Gampel Pavilion before a sellout crowd of 8,241 and a national ESPN audience.

For Tennessee, this kind of attention had been part of the routine for years. There were three national titles on the resume and the Lady Vols

had advanced to the NCAA or Association of Intercollegiate Athletics for Women Final Four 11 times in the previous 18 years. In fact, Tennessee had played in 12 games involving Nos. 1 and 2 and won seven.

Still, the team's 16-0 start was the best ever for coach Pat Summitt in 21 seasons. Summitt had the luxury of choosing among 12 high school All-Americans, one of the reasons

Against Tennessee, Kim Better, Missy Rose and Pam Webber see what it takes to be No. 1 in the country for the first time.

BRAD CLIFT PHOTO

Tennessee had beaten nine teams ranked 13th or higher, six of them on the road.

Both teams came out pressing mercilessly and Tennessee took a 6-5 lead before UConn exerted itself. Rebecca Lobo's three-point shot and a three-point play by guard Jennifer Rizzotti started a 10-0 run that gave the Huskies a 15-6 lead they never relinquished.

UConn confused the quicker Tennessee team by switching defenses and led 41-33 at halftime. Almost inevitably, Tennessee climbed back into the game. Lobo, in foul trouble, retired to the bench. Senior center Dana Johnson dropped in two layups and the UConn lead was a tenuous 58-53 with 9

Nobody likes to be labeled but in the case of this fan, Meg Nobel, UConn will make an exception. That is the reward for the kind of team that coach Geno Auriemma, below, would never allow to simply go through the motions.

BRAD CLIFT PHOTOS

minutes, 19 seconds left. Geno Auriemma, who sensed a trace of anxiety in his team, immediately called a timeout.

"Some of the calls were going the other way, and I could see in their eyes and their body language that there started to be a little doubt," Auriemma said later. "There was a little apprehension, like, 'Uh-oh, here they come. Now they're playing their A game.' "

Auriemma quietly explained that UConn had worked just as hard as Tennessee had in the practices and games leading to this meeting of irresistible force and immovable object. Point well taken.

Lobo re-entered the game and set up a basket by Kara Wolters. After two free throws by Wolters, Lobo made a

Missy Rose lets Rebecca Lobo know she appreciates where UConn's volume of work has taken it during a victory against Tennessee.

BRAD CLIFT PHOTO

steal off a rebound and laid in the ball for a 64-53 lead with 7:43 left. When Lobo fouled out with 4:52 left, the score was 69-57. Before leaving the floor, she gathered her teammates at midcourt.

"I told Kara to post up hard, I told Jamelle [Elliott] to get every rebound," Lobo said. "I'm sure they didn't hear a single word I said, and I really don't care because they just played unbelievable."

As the clock ran out, Lobo sat on the bench whispering to herself, "One, one, one." When the buzzer sounded, Elliott hurled the basketball straight up — the exclamation point on UConn's biggest victory.

The scoreboard read: UConn 77, Tennessee 66.

Lobo led the charge toward the players on the court with her arms extended and index fingers pointing up. They all wound up on the floor in a pile while television cameras and photographers recorded the glorious scene.

"We had more Connecticut than we could handle," Summitt said. "Rebecca Lobo is the most versatile post player we've faced and brings lots of confidence to their team. But they're just not Rebecca Lobo, and I think they understand that. It's probably good for them to play and win without her down the stretch."

Lobo, playing with a broken right pinky wrapped in a protective splint, produced 13 points, eight rebounds and five blocked shots. She had support from all quarters:

• Rizzotti had 17 points, five steals and four assists. Moreover, she protected the ball well in the face of Tennessee's pressure. She played 39 minutes and was the pivotal player. After the game, Auriemma called her the best point guard in America.

Jennifer Rizzotti has her own direction and will keep on driving until she creates for UConn, as Tennessee's Michelle Marciniak can attest.

BRAD CLIFT PHOTO

• Wolters hit some big baskets and scored a game-high 18 points and had five blocks.

• UConn's defense forced the Lady Vols into 25 turnovers and held Nikki McCray and Michelle Marciniak to a combined 7-for-24 from the field.

And though UConn matched its lowest point total of the season and had its third-lowest shooting percentage (46.8), the team had survived a very stern test. The Huskies were 13-0 and working on a home winning streak of 28 games, third-longest in the nation.

With one minute left, delirious fans began to chant "We're No. 1. We're No. 1." Indeed, for the first time, the UConn women's basketball team would be ranked first in the entire country.

There was no doubt in anyone's mind.

Even Summitt, who lingered on the court to chat with fans and sign autographs, acknowledged the obvious.

Asked if UConn deserved to be No. 1, she nodded and said, "They got my vote." ■

After a victory over Tennessee, the country knows what Rebecca Lobo, far left, and UConn are up to. Lobo and coach Geno Auriemma, above, embrace as they fulfill the quest for a No. 1 ranking.

ALBERT DICKSON PHOTOS

As Chapter Four ends: UConn is 13-0 and about to be ranked No. 1.

*With one minute left,
delirious fans
began to chant
"We're No. 1.
We're No. 1."
Indeed, for
the first time,
the UConn women's
basketball team
would be
ranked first
in the entire country.
There was no doubt
in anyone's mind.*

UConn prepares to fall
into the role of No. 1 team
in the nation,
a title that belonged
to the Huskies
one day after stopping
the Vols.

BRAD CLIFT PHOTO

■ CHAPTER FIVE

Auriemma shows some fight

E xhilarating as it was to be the nation's top-ranked women's basketball team, the UConn Huskies quickly discovered that recognition comes with a price. In a word, pressure. From the outside, and from within.

When William Shakespeare wrote, *"Uneasy lies the head that wears a crown,"* he was describing Henry IV's nervous reign. Two days after an emphatic victory over Tennessee, one day after UConn was voted No. 1 in the Associated Press poll, those words clearly captured coach Geno Auriemma.

You could almost see the valley coming after the Huskies defeated the Lady Volunteers. The opponent Jan. 18 was Boston College and the venue Conte Forum, where a record crowd of 2,415 gathered,

Jan. 18
UConn 79
Boston College 54

Jan. 22
UConn 89
Syracuse 58

Jan. 24
UConn 92
Miami 51

(Box scores, Page 134)

hoping for a miracle. It did get something extraordinary:

• Auriemma received his second technical foul of the season for complaining about BC's rough play. After the game, in harsh terms, he criticized Eagles coach Cathy Inglese and officials John Jones and Janice Aliberti for tolerating "chippy" play.

• UConn, playing sloppily, was outscored 30-28 in the second half.

• For the first time in 14 games, freshman Nykesha Sales failed to score in double figures.

That the Huskies won with ease 79-54 and moved to 14-0 was almost completely lost in the wreckage of Auriemma's postgame comments. And it wasn't a throwaway line or two, it was a scathing monologue:

"I just think it was a chippy kind of game where it was how many people can you smash and grab for the next 12 minutes," Auriemma told reporters. "I don't want to tell anyone how to coach, but if I was one of their kids sitting on the end of the bench in a 30-point loss I wouldn't be too happy.

"So if you want to write that it was sloppy, yeah, it

Against Boston College, coach Geno Auriemma heads in the wrong direction, in the opinion of Janice Aliberti, who gives him a technical. After the game, Auriemma said he disapproved of BC's "chippy" play.

RICHARD MESSINA
PHOTOS

was. But there was a reason it was sloppy. When you put bad players and bad officials together, that's the kind of game you get. I'm really sick and tired of the kind of officiating we've been getting. It's not fair to these kids."

There was more:
"We always were a target because we've been No. 1 in this league for years. I don't mind being a target because that makes our guys play hard. But when your intent is to just go out there and push Rebecca Lobo around, that's not basketball."

And: "I'm not crying. We just played the most physical team in the country, and I didn't say boo. But there's a difference between playing physical and being chippy. Anyone who watched the game knows what I'm talking about."

Not surprisingly, Inglese did not agree. "I can certainly understand Geno getting frustrated,

Associate head coach Chris Dailey, far right, came to UConn with Geno Auriemma in 1985 and concentrates on everything from recruiting to the occasional pep talk, as is the case with Kara Wolters, above.

MICHAEL KODAS AND RICHARD MESSINA PHOTOS

but I think it was going both ways," she said. "We don't normally play that physical. To be honest, I wish every game we played that physical, where we bump and bang a little bit.

"No, we don't usually do that, but because they play such an inside game we were forced into a situation to really hold our own.
I think the difference being, as my assistant says, that UConn bumps and bangs with a little bit more finesse — we don't look as nice doing it."

The game was certifiably rough; there were flurries of elbows — when Pam Webber was felled by one from BC's Kinzer Cohen, Auriemma's protest drew a technical. Late in the first half, the Eagles' Holly Porter slapped Kara Wolters in the face while they fought for a rebound. Wolters responded by throwing Porter to the floor.

Even if Auriemma's rage was justified, there is an unwritten code in sports that coaches do not openly question officiating. And, there was the not-so-small

Kara Wolters (52), right, helps put another game out of reach, this time with 10 points and two blocks against Miami and Octavia Blue.

Wolters, far right, has become used to doing some of the heavy lifting for the team.

RICHARD MESSINA
AND
SHERRY PETERS
PHOTOS

matter of the Big East's written policy regarding such behavior.

Maura Legere, director of championship services for the conference, heard Auriemma's outburst and circulated copies of the Big East code of conduct, which forbids public criticism of officials, coaches and players.

Auriemma apologized to Inglese the following day, and she accepted.

After meeting with Auriemma, UConn president Harry Hartley and athletic director Lew Perkins reprimanded the coach publicly. Privately, the two were believed to have put Auriemma on notice by placing this ultimatum in his personnel file: do it again and risk losing your job.

Big East commissioner Mike Tranghese said he approved of the penalty, which was more severe than anything that would have been imposed by the conference. "If it happens again, I think it

would be a suspension of a significant magnitude," Tranghese said. "But I don't think it will happen again."

When Auriemma walked onto the court at Gampel Pavilion Jan. 22, he was greeted with a standing ovation from the sellout of 8,241. The coach did not critique the officiating during or after the game. Rather, he prodded UConn to an 89-58 victory, the team's 15th without a loss and the 23rd in a row in the Big East, a conference record.

Eight minutes into the game, UConn went on a 19-0 run and pressed Syracuse into submission. On defense, Syracuse stood back in its two-three zone and dared the Huskies to shoot from the perimeter. Point guard Jennifer Rizzotti, who managed six of UConn's season-high 17 steals, added a game-high 19 points and six assists.

Carla Berube, starting her first game of the season, scored nine points, along with Jamelle Elliott and Sales. Coming off the bench, Wolters scored 14 points.

Two nights later, in Coral Gables, Fla., top-ranked UConn easily improved to 16-0. The score against Miami was 92-51 and, as usual,

Against Miami and Octavia Blue, the output of Jamelle Elliott had yet to fall off and after the 16th consecutive victory, UConn was set to face Kansas.

RICHARD MESSINA PHOTO

the Huskies' points came from a variety of places.

Webber, for instance, had scored in double figures only once in 30 previous games, but reeled off 10 in a span of 133 seconds in the first half. The senior co-captain scored 14 points and had two assists — with no turnovers — in 25 minutes.

Lobo scored 17 points, but missed 15 of 21 shots.

UConn now had won a record 24 consecutive Big East games, but the next opponent was hardly the comforting, known quantity of a Miami or a Syracuse. In what promised to be their toughest road game of the season and the biggest remaining obstacle to an undefeated regular season, the Huskies prepared to travel to Kansas City and a long-awaited men's and women's doubleheader between UConn and Kansas. ■

As Chapter Five ends:
UConn is 16-0 and ranked No. 1.

■ CHAPTER SIX

The Kansas test

Jan. 28
UConn 97
Kansas 87

*(Box score,
Page 135)*

asketball is omnipotent at the University of Kansas, something pervasive and yet almost unconscious. Kind of like breathing. It was Dr. James Naismith, seven years removed from his experimental peach baskets at Springfield College, who brought his new game to the school. That was in 1898. Phog Allen and Adolph Rupp coached there, Wilt Chamberlain and Dean Smith played there.

When the men's and women's doubleheader between Kansas and UConn was announced before the season, certainly it had delicious possibilities. But then, as the four teams marched through their schedules with very little problem, the tradition-fed fans in Kansas and the people of Connecticut began to plan their social calendars around Saturday, Jan. 28.

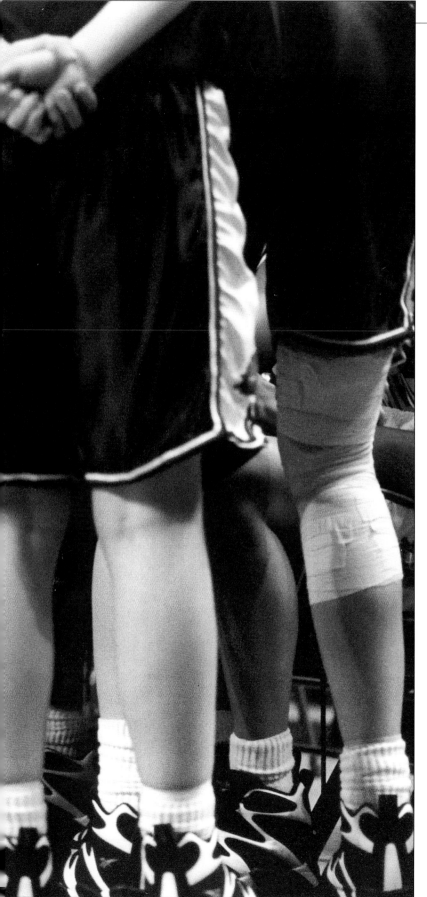

That was the day the Kansas women's team, ranked 17th in the nation, played the top-ranked and undefeated UConn women on CBS. Later, the undefeated UConn men, ranked second, faced No. 7 Kansas. The games were at Kemper Arena in Kansas City, Mo., about an hour down I-70 from the Kansas campus in Lawrence, Kan.

On the surface, anyway, the UConn men seemed to face the more difficult proposition. Geno Auriemma wasn't so sure. The UConn women's coach knew Kansas was 22-6 the year before and returned seven letter-winners and three starters, including senior forward Angela Aycock.

Privately, Auriemma worried about his team's performance under duress. UConn (16-0) had not suffered a great deal of adversity. Even including the test against Tennessee, the average margin of victory was 38.6 points.

In a position such as coach Geno Auriemma's, against an opponent such as Kansas, it is important that everything match perfectly.

BRAD CLIFT PHOTO

The game began with about half the 16,981 seats at Kemper occupied, but by the end, there was a capacity crowd. The fans saw a terrific game.

Early, the game was a battle of frontliners, with Aycock scoring 13 of her team's first 16 points. UConn's Rebecca Lobo countered with 12 points in the first 12 minutes. Despite an 11-0 Kansas run, the Huskies led, 28-24.

UConn's Nykesha Sales, who had been in a three-game slump, began to produce. She had scored in double figures in each of her first 13 games, but had fallen off to three consecutive games in single digits. Now, after a long talk with her parents and Auriemma, Sales was shooting three-pointers — and hitting them. She made three in the first half. The second began a 19-9 UConn run that helped build a 47-35 halftime lead.

From there, the UConn lead

expanded and contracted frenetically:

Pam Webber's three-pointer gave the Huskies a 54-41 lead with 17 minutes, 45 seconds left, but Kansas worked it down to 63-58. A layup and two free throws by Lobo and another three-pointer by Sales put UConn up by a comfortable 76-63 with 9:02 left. It was 83-70 with 5:40 left, when Kansas made it a little scary.

Sophomore Tamecka Dixon scored seven of Kansas' next 12 points to bring the Jayhawks to 86-82. Now, Auriemma and the critics would see how the Huskies responded in a tight game.

Quite well, thank you.

After UConn called a timeout with 2:18 left, Kara Wolters took a feed from Carla Berube, but Kansas' Angie Halbleib made two free throws with 1:55 left. And then UConn buried the Jayhawks with six free throws (by Berube, Wolters and Jennifer

Rebecca Lobo, far left, poked in the eye by Kansas' Angela Aycock, was not seriously injured and again became the focus, scoring 25 points on 9-for-17 shooting and finishing with 12 rebounds.

MICHAEL McANDREWS
AND
BRAD CLIFT
PHOTOS

Rizzotti) and an offensive follow by Wolters.

The final, 97-87, in no way represented the game's intensity.

"I was proud to see that from this team," Auriemma said, "because so many times we've had to answer the questions, 'How good are you when you're winning every game by 40?' or 'What's going to happen when you get tested?'

"Well, I think they answered that. When Kansas made its run, we had an answer, didn't get too flustered and were able to make the big plays we had to make at the end."

I n the end, UConn's best player was superb. Lobo had 25 points and 12 rebounds. Rizzotti and Sales each had 21 points. For Kansas, Dixon scored a career-high 30 points and Aycock 29. Along with Charisse Sampson (19 points), the three scored 66 of Kansas' first 70 points.

Rebecca Lobo, left, didn't finish higher in points than Kansas' Tamecka Dixon but Lobo and the Huskies did land another victory.

Far right: After struggling for three games, Nykesha Sales, determined to break out of her slump, scored 21 points against Kansas.

BRAD CLIFT PHOTOS

Kansas coach Marian Washington described her team's strategy: "We realized, even against Tennessee, they shot a lot of layups, so in the first half we tried to force them to shoot outside and cut off their inside game. In the second half, we wanted to test our ability to go full court, and I thought we created some pressure, then got a little tired. We gave up a lot of height, and every time we made a run they got an easy layup."

Lobo seemed relieved after the game. "I wouldn't say we were looking for a close game, but if at any point we thought it was slipping away, it would have slipped away," she said. "I think we responded well and held up under pressure.

"It will only help us down the line."

The UConn men were routed by Kansas in the second game 88-59 and suddenly the UConn women were alone. Of the 595 teams that played Division I basketball, only one had yet to lose. ■

As Chapter Six ends:
UConn is 17-0 and ranked No. 1.

*"When
Kansas made
its run,
we had
an answer,
didn't get
too flustered
and were able
to make the
big plays
we had
to make
at the end."*

• UConn coach
Geno Auriemma

Pam Webber, left,
Rebecca Lobo, back,
Jennifer Rizzotti (21)
and Carla Berube had
a collective 58 points
and 17 assists
vs. Kansas.

MICHAEL McANDREWS PHOTO

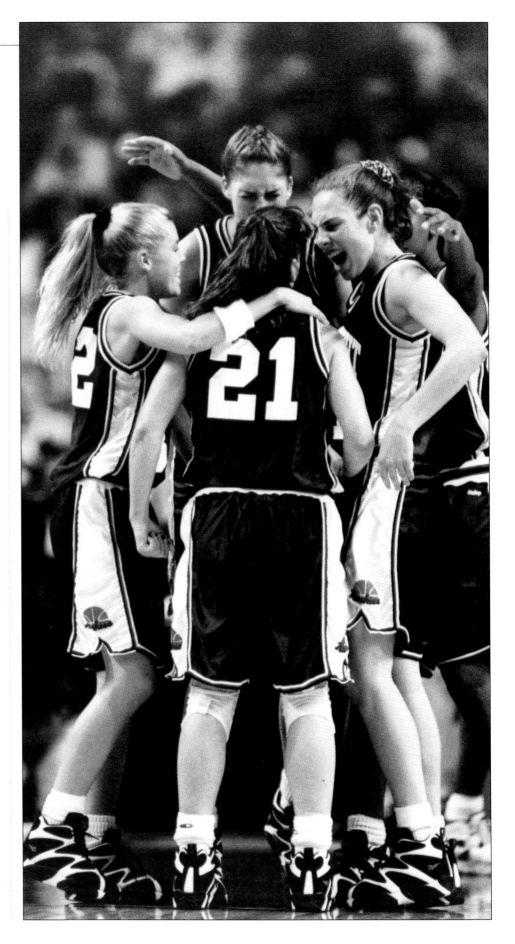

■ CHAPTER SEVEN

Can't ask for more

The electricity of the Kansas victory wore off soon enough. Now, coach Geno Auriemma wondered to himself, how do I keep this team focused? It was a valid question because UConn's nine remaining games were against Big East opponents the Huskies had beaten badly.

"How do you keep everybody emotionally and psychologically together?" he asked a week later. "How do you keep that bubble around your team? Because now the chinks start coming out."

The fears, in retrospect, were unfounded.

Providence actually led 30-19 on Jan. 31 but eventually lost, 89-56.

Georgetown lost 94-72, largely because of Rebecca Lobo's career-high 33 points.

Jan. 31
UConn 89
Providence 56

Feb. 5
UConn 94
Georgetown 72

Feb. 9
UConn 85
Miami 48

Feb. 12
UConn 84
Seton Hall 62

Feb. 16
UConn 71
Pittsburgh 43

Feb. 19
UConn 86
Boston College 34

Feb. 22
UConn 103
St. John's 56

Feb. 25
UConn 89
Syracuse 62

Feb. 27
UConn 79
Villanova 54

(Box scores, Pages 135-138)

Miami was defeated 85-48 as Lobo had 19 points, 11 rebounds and eight blocks.

Seton Hall didn't take advantage of UConn's foul trouble and lost, 84-62.

Pittsburgh, unable to stop Lobo (26 points) and Kara Wolters (13), lost, 71-43.

Boston College was routed 86-34 Feb. 19.

Three nights later at Gampel Pavilion, UConn's three seniors played their last regular season home game. Listed in the starting lineup against St. John's were co-captains Lobo and Pam Webber, as well as walk-on Jill Gelfenbien, the goalie for the soccer team that reached the Final Four.

Lobo and Webber were high school seniors during the UConn women's breakthrough 1990-91 season, which included a 29-5 record and a trip to the Final Four in New Orleans. They met

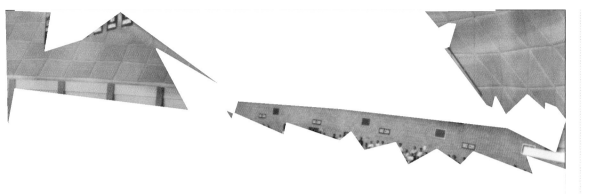

when their recruiting visits to Storrs coincided, and became roommates. Four years later, they were best friends. In four years at UConn their record was an astonishing 95-25, a winning percentage of .792.

The game was on Connecticut Public Television, the ninth time CPTV televised one of the women's games. The pregame ceremony was, artistically and emotionally speaking, the highlight of the evening.

The three seniors were introduced along with their parents and presented with framed replicas of their uniforms. The sellout crowd of 8,241 was moved.

"Everyone was crying," said Wolters, a sophomore. "I think it kind of hit us that Rebecca, Pam and Jill have done so much for every one of us. I don't even want to think what it's going to be like without them, but we still have so much of the season.

"It's sad and happy at the same time, but they're not gone yet."

For what seemed to be the longest time, they might as well have been. Lobo threw up an air ball and Gelfenbien missed a nervous, 4-foot jump shot before the Huskies settled. A layup by Lobo finally started UConn on its way to a 103-56 victory.

"The ceremonies were really something I can't describe," said Lobo, who finished with 13 points, 16 rebounds and seven blocks. "It was very emotional because this has been a special place for us the past four years, but the crowd showed why we like playing here so much. They're so unbelievable, and we can't thank them enough."

Auriemma wasn't surprised by the Huskies' slow start. "I knew they can shoot with hands in their face," Auriemma said,

"but I didn't know if they could score with tears in their eyes."

Huddling after the game as "We Are the Champions" played, the Huskies donned T-shirts reading "Back 2 Back Big East Regular Season Champions," then saluted the fans as the band played the school fight song.

It was a memorable curtain call.

"It felt funny going back on the court, but it was pretty special to have clinched it on our court because all the supporters got to see it," said Webber, the shooting guard who added nine points and four assists. "They were outstanding with all the standing ovations."

The Huskies were 24-0 and Big East champions for the second consecutive year. It was time to get back to business.

Syracuse, on Feb. 25, was dismissed, 89-62.

And now, a single regular season

Here is part of the word from the stands at Gampel from an avowed Pam Webber fan, far left, during a victory over St. John's Feb. 22.

With the play of senior guard Pam Webber (32) against Boston College, UConn continues to reach new ground.

SHERRY PETERS
AND
PAULA BRONSTEIN
PHOTOS

game remained. Two 20-minute halves separated the UConn women from history. They stood a breathless 25-0, 17-0 in the Big East. In the eight conference games since defeating Kansas, the average score had been – UConn 88, Big East 54.

The lead in The Hartford Courant on Feb. 27 read:

"Miami Dolphins. Don Larsen. Torvill and Dean. Nadia Comaneci. UCLA.

"Perfection.

"The No. 1 UConn women get a shot at it tonight."

A victory over Villanova, the second-best team in the conference, on the road at duPont Pavilion would enable the Huskies to become the first Big East team, men's or women's, to complete the regular season undefeated.

From left: Brenda Marquis, Rebecca Lobo, Kelley Hunt and Kara Wolters dance with teammates to "We Are the Champions" after winning the Big East title with a victory over St. John's.

It ended as a 103-56 victory over St. John's but Geno Auriemma, below, still wants to walk his team through a few things beforehand.

PAULA BRONSTEIN
PHOTOS

Sophomore Carla Berube, right, is able to get ahold of 13 points in 18 minutes against Miami.

Jennifer Rizzotti, far right, drives past Seton Hall's Sandy Mitchell, toward an undefeated season, scoring 18 points in 37 minutes.

With the play of Nykesha Sales (42) – 15 points, four steals – another game gets out of hand for a UConn opponent, this time Seton Hall.

BRAD CLIFT AND ALBERT DICKSON PHOTOS

"The only people who really understand what we're trying to do or what it means to be going for an undefeated season, are people who have really accomplished something," Auriemma said a day before the game. "People, like the president of Travelers and Aetna, will sit in their offices and say, 'You know, I can relate to this because I know how hard it is to get on top and stay there.'

"**E**very time we play, it's the other guy's big shot, like Syracuse Saturday. They lost, but if they played like they did against us all the time, they wouldn't be [7-19], they'd be third or fourth in the league.

"If we win, people might say this t say is the best team in the history of the the Big East."

It was with that grand backdrop that UConn's women took the floor for the Monday night regular season finale. There

As UConn
continues to be
one of the
first names
in women's
basketball,
Missy Rose
greets Caitlin
Purcell, 10,
and her brother,
Colin, 5 months,
of Mystic,
before Rose
autographs
a hat for Caitlin.

PAULA BRONSTEIN
PHOTO

were a regular season record 3,622 in the seats at duPont. Some were from nearby Norristown, Pa., where Auriemma grew up. They included his parents, Donato and Marsiella, his brother Ferruccio and sister Anna.

They watched in awe as their son and brother guided UConn into uncharted territory. The Huskies beat Villanova 79-54 and:

• Became the first conference team of either gender to complete a regular season unbeaten (26-0).

• Joined the 1991-92 Miami women as the only other Big East team to go undefeated (18-0) in conference play.

• Set a Big East record with a 35-1 record over back-to-back seasons.

There were more glories of an individual nature:

Wolters, the 6-foot-7 center, made 12 of 17 shots and scored a career-high 26 points. Point guard Jennifer Rizzotti scored eight points and finished with 1,003 in her UConn career, becoming the 11th UConn woman to reach 1,000. Lobo finished her Big East regular season career first in rebounds (714) and blocks (227) and fourth in scoring (1,232 points). Webber, who had never missed a practice or game, played in her 122nd game, third all-time at UConn.

Through all the exhilaration only one question

Within the framework of the season came a ceremony honoring seniors Rebecca Lobo, Pam Webber and Jill Gelfenbien. Geno Auriemma, Lobo and her mother, RuthAnn, take part Feb. 22.

buzzed along the borders of the subconscious: Would all these blowouts hurt the Huskies' ability to concentrate at tournament time, when games and teams get a little tighter?

Auriemma, in his typically straight-ahead fashion, addressed the issue after the game.

"Being 26-0 isn't something we had consciously thought of when the season started, but we won them all," he said. "I've heard all the stories about the league we play in and the schedule we play, so I guess we get a chance to prove ourselves next weekend [in the Big East tournament] and in the NCAAs.

"But for now, we don't have to prove anything to anyone. We've done what very few teams can do, and I'm really proud of my players." ■

As Chapter Seven ends:
UConn is 26-0, Big East regular season champion and ranked No. 1.

■ CHAPTER EIGHT

How does 29-0 sound?

*Big East tournament
(South Orange, N.J.)*

March 4
UConn 92
Providence 63

March 5
UConn 95
Pittsburgh 63

March 6
UConn 85
Seton Hall 49

*(Box scores,
Pages 138-139)*

Conn came to Seton Hall's Walsh Gymnasium as the overwhelming favorite to win its second consecutive Big East tournament title and a record fourth overall.

Walsh had been the site of UConn's last Big East loss, 74-53 to the Pirates 14 months earlier, but that didn't trouble the Huskies as they prepared for their March 4 game against Providence. The Friars, on the other hand, left them a little nervous.

It was a fearless Providence team that attempted enough three-pointers to lead UConn by 11 points Jan. 31. The Huskies recovered from the season's largest deficit to win 89-56, but a lesson was learned.

"We wanted to start with even more intensity than

usual to set the tone for the rest of the weekend," said point guard Jennifer Rizzotti. "Providence is a streaky team — when they get on fire they can really hit some shots — and we wanted to make sure we took them out of the game plan right from the beginning."

Less than nine minutes into the game, UConn led, 30-9. The final was 92-63. The Huskies shot a season-high 67.7 percent in the first half (21-for-31) and 58.5 for the game.

Forward Rebecca Lobo had 23 points, 12 rebounds and three blocked shots.

UConn met Pittsburgh in the March 5 semifinals and this time center Kara Wolters (25) and Lobo totaled 45 points, mostly from inside. The final was 95-63 and the Huskies were 28-0. Coach Geno Auriemma, whose level of expectation had grown dangerously high as the

Left, Geno Auriemma, his son, Michael, and daughter Alysa, and Rebecca Lobo, above, ready for the Big East tournament opener.

UConn focuses,
far right, before
a tournament
victory over
Pittsburgh that
was never
on the line
for Rebecca
Lobo, above, and
her teammates.

ALBERT DICKSON
PHOTOS

season progressed,
seemed a little down
after the game.

"It was ugly, it wasn't
pretty," he said. "Every
game can't be exactly
the way I want them to
be. But at this time of
year you don't get any
points on how good you
look. You just win and
keep on going."

UConn faced Seton
Hall (23-7), playing on
its home court, in the
championship final.

"The emotion and
intensity in the locker
room before the game
was kind of electric," Lobo said. "Our play
was a result of that."

Seton Hall's Tahnee Heins
controlled the opening tap and
drove for an uncontested layup,
but the ball rolled off the rim. It
was the first of 10 consecutive missed shots
by the Pirates. Meanwhile, UConn led,
10-0.

With Seton Hall committed to double-
teaming Lobo, wherever she played,

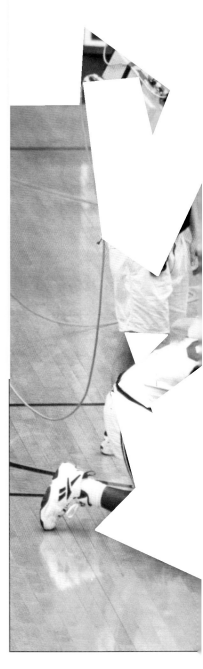

Wolters was left to contend with the Pirates' 6-foot-3 center Dawn Johnson. It was no match. Wolters had a free hand most of the night, but even when she drew two defenders in the second half, she managed to score.

The Huskies' largest lead, 85-39, came well after Wolters had retired to the bench. By that time she had a career-high 32 points.

The score was a comfortable 85-49 and it set off a prolonged celebration, on the court and in the packed stands.

"They were just awesome," said Auriemma in the crowded interview room. "I can't think of anybody who didn't play really well."

A television reporter asked: "Was that 40 minutes of perfect basketball?"

Auriemma smiled and shook his head.

"No. No," he said. "Don't fill their heads up with that stuff."

Auriemma talked about the presence of Lobo and Rizzotti, saying that a number of good teams have a versatile forward and a strong point guard. "But," Auriemma said, "nobody else has anything like Kara."

Consider the low-post wreckage that Wolters wrought in three games and 73 minutes: 76 points, 16 blocks and 14 rebounds.

Moreover, Wolters made 34 of 45 shots (75.6 percent). She was chosen the tournament's Most

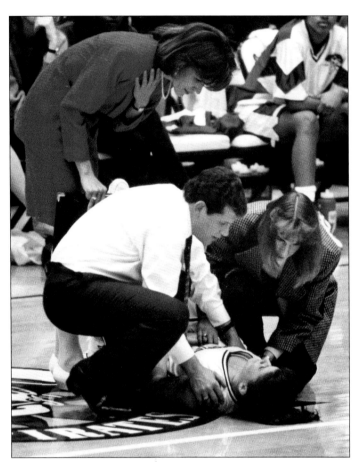

After injuring
her right elbow
against Seton Hall,
Jennifer Rizzotti is helped
off the court, far right,
by athletic trainer
Alicia Blake and
associate coach
Chris Dailey, right.

PAULA BRONSTEIN
AND
ALBERT DICKSON
PHOTOS

Outstanding Player, which went to Lobo the year before.

Lobo, who joined Wolters on the All-Tournament team, had some tidy three-game totals herself: 58 points, 32 rebounds and 10 blocks. Lobo produced double figures in scoring and rebounding in each game.

Freshman Nykesha Sales was the third Husky player to make the All-Tournament team. Her three-game totals (averaging 20 minutes a game): 30 points, 17 rebounds, 16 steals and 14 assists.

In fact, Sales set the tournament record for steals. The previous record was 11.

The only downside was a tendon injury to Rizzotti's right elbow after a collision with Seton Hall's Heins. Rizzotti left the game early in the second half but vowed to be ready for the NCAA Tournament 10 days later.

Nonetheless, with two steals in the first half, Rizzotti set the school's single-season steals record with 87, one more than Debbie Baer.

The Huskies broke four of their own Big East tournament records that had been set the year before: total margin of victory (97 points), team steals (44), team blocks (28), team assists (82).

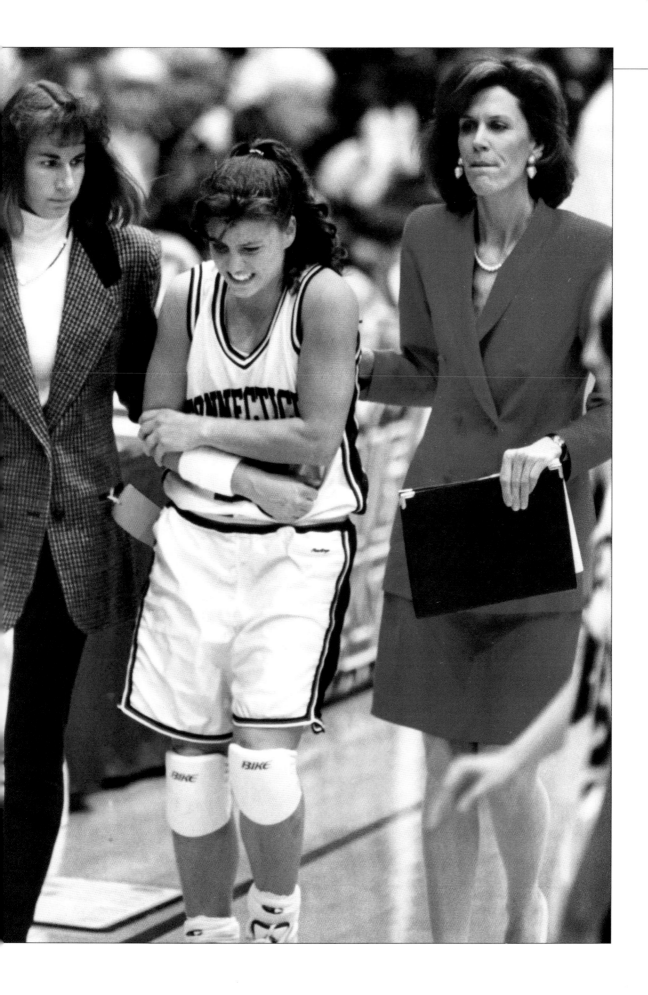

Nykesha Sales
helps Kara Wolters,
at right, adjust
a contact.

Far right:
Rebecca Lobo
and Jennifer Rizzotti
pulled together
to beat Seton Hall
and win
the conference
tournament.
Lobo, Wolters
and Sales
were selected
to the
All-Tournament
team.

PAULA BRONSTEIN PHOTOS

The spoils of victory extended beyond Big East records. By finishing 29-0, UConn became only the sixth women's team in history to enter tournament play undefeated. The others: Oral Roberts (24-0 in NAIA, 1983), Texas (29-0, 1986), Louisiana Tech (29-0, 1990), Vermont (29-0, 1992 and 28-0, 1993). Only Texas was able to win the NCAA title and finish unbeaten (34-0).

With the news that Tennessee had lost to Vanderbilt 67-61 in the Southeastern Conference championship game came the guarantee that UConn's eight-week reign as the nation's top-ranked team would extend to the final Associated Press poll. UConn was a unanimous No. 1.

After the game, Seton Hall coach Phyllis Mangina

talked about the emergence of Wolters and wondered if anyone would beat the Huskies.

"Who's going to stop a 6-foot-7 player on a baby hook?" she said. "You've got to be kidding me.

"If she plays that well, and Lobo's in there and Rizzotti's firing three-pointers and you have Sales on the wing … I don't know who is going to defend them. When they get on a roll like that, they are absolutely the best team in the country." ∎

As Chapter Eight ends:
UConn is 29-0, Big East tournament champion and ranked No. 1.

EIGHT

Rebecca Lobo
(58 points
in three tournament
games) and
Geno Auriemma,
a tournament title
in their grasp,
can enjoy
the moment.

ALBERT DICKSON PHOTO

"If [Wolters] plays that well, and Lobo's in there and Rizzotti's firing three-pointers and you have Sales on the wing ... When they get on a roll like that, they are absolutely the best team in the country."

• Seton Hall coach Phyllis Mangina

Rebecca Lobo, left, and Pam Webber helped lift UConn to a school tournament record for total margin of victory (97 points).

ALBERT DICKSON PHOTO

■ CHAPTER NINE

For two, Stephen King ending

NCAA
Tournament
First & second
rounds
(Gampel Pavilion,
Storrs)

March 16
UConn 105
Maine 75

March 18
UConn 91
Virginia Tech 45

(Box scores,
Page 139)

As if the University of Maine women's basketball team didn't have enough to worry about. Even as the 16th-seeded Black Bears were practicing at Gampel Pavilion for their East Regional game with top-seeded UConn, the news arrived that three Huskies had been chosen All-Americans.

Only two UConn players in history — Kerry Bascom and Rebecca Lobo — had ever been named, but in a single day, the total increased to a rather formidable five selections. Lobo, a senior, was named to the first team and appeared on every ballot. Junior point guard Jennifer Rizzotti made the second team and sophomore center Kara Wolters the third team.

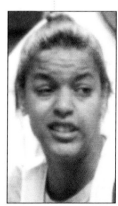

And so Maine entered the March 16 game insecure

in the knowledge that the team it would try to beat started three of the nation's best 15 players.

The Black Bears had some local talent working in their favor; freshman Cindy Blodgett was the most prolific high school player in Maine history, with 2,596 points and a frightening average of 36.4. Novelist Stephen King, a Bangor resident, attended the game with his wife, Tabitha, but, for Maine, it turned very quickly into one of his nightmares.

Blodgett had been recruited by UConn coach Geno Auriemma, but was unimpressed with Auriemma's low-key approach and was quoted as saying so in a Maine newspaper before the game.

Kim Better works against a well-manned defense before the women opened the NCAA Tournament with a game against Maine at Gampel Pavilion. The women often practice against male players, from left, Matt McCorry, Mark Shaker and Kyle Chapman.

SHERRY PETERS PHOTO

After 20 minutes, if Blodgett wasn't impressed with Auriemma's team, she wasn't paying attention. Maine's point guard, looking tentative, made only 1 of 7 shots in the first half and scored two points.

The Huskies, meanwhile, led 53-25 at the half and showed no rust after a 10-day layoff. Lobo, who had memories of slow starts in years past, made two three-pointers in the first 53 seconds. The Huskies were never seriously challenged. Auriemma's liberal substitutions allowed Maine to score 50 points in the second half, but UConn won 105-75 Thursday night, the seventh time at 100 or more points this season.

The victory at sold-out Gampel started more statistical mayhem. The Huskies set school single-game NCAA Tournament records for:

• Margin of victory (30 points, breaking the record of 22 vs. Auburn in 1994).

• Points scored (105, vs. 83 against St. Peter's in 1992), most rebounds (56, vs. 52 against Southern Miss in 1994), most assists (27, vs. 26 against

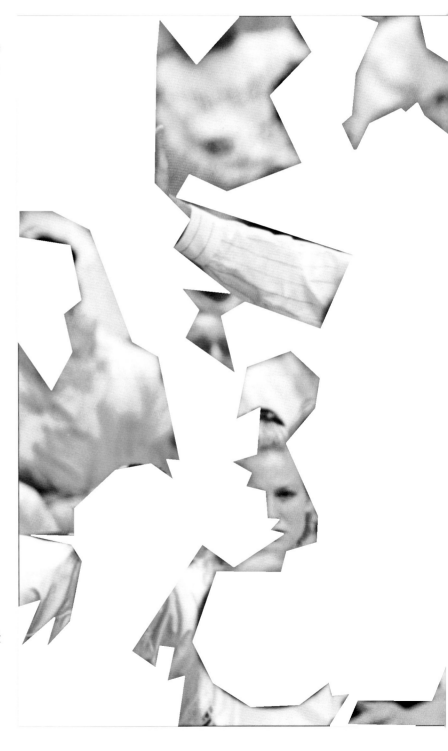

Geno Auriemma sees what the widest NCAA Tournament victory margin in school history (30 points, vs. Maine) says about his team. The Huskies' point total (105) also was a UConn tournament record.

PAULA BRONSTEIN PHOTO

North Carolina in 1994), best three-point field-goal percentage (.615, vs. .563 against N.C. State in 1991).

"I was a little bit concerned going into the game because it's been our history — the layoff can cause us to play a little skittish," Auriemma said. "But the first 10 minutes of the second half . . . I don't think we can play much better than that."

UConn was 30-0. The coaches, who watched Virginia Tech grind past St. Joseph's in the first game 62-52, almost immediately started viewing videotape in preparation for their Saturday game.

Virginia Tech coach Carol Alfano did not exactly sound intimidated about the prospect of playing UConn. "We have been in some big games," Alfano said. "We beat Virginia, played North Carolina close and lost to Tennessee. I think we'll show up."

Even in the postgame press conference, Virginia Tech star Jenny Root telegraphed her team's game plan. "I don't think I'll be venturing inside too often," said the 6-foot-3 center. "They're really tall."

UConn's 91-45, second-round victory over Virginia Tech was astonishingly easy. "It's like the old country-western song," said Alfano of her 22-9 team.

As UConn takes
a 53-25 halftime lead
against Maine,
from left,
Rebecca Lobo,
Geno Auriemma
and Missy Rose
help ensure
that the Huskies'
emotional level
is heightened
from the bench.

At right, novelist
Stephen King cheers
on Maine, his home
state team.

SHERRY PETERS PHOTOS

"Sometimes you're the windshield, sometimes you're the bug. We were the bug."

T he Huskies squashed the Hokies with such vigor that the highlight was a moving personal moment for Jamelle Elliott. Of all UConn's starters, the junior forward was by far the least appreciated. All she did was average 10 points and eight rebounds. She was not an All-American, but her teammates agreed she helped them achieve that status.

Which is why they were pulling so hard for her on the free-throw line with 7 minutes, 59 seconds left. "COME ON, JAMELLE!" Rizzotti urged as Elliott stepped forward. Rizzotti and Lobo had checked with the team managers and they knew Elliott had 999 career points. After the overstated encouragement of her teammates, Elliott knew, too.

The first free throw barely grazed the front rim.

Geri White of Hampton, right, is part of the animated crowd as UConn routs Virginia Tech, while, below, a doll owned by Christine Gelinas, 8, of Vernon, is a tribute to Pam Webber's style.

With Auriemma shouting, "This is for the thousandth! This is for the thousandth!" she made the second free throw. Elliott had become only the 12th UConn woman to score 1,000 points. Elliott received a standing ovation and was surrounded by her teammates for a group hug.

"I'm glad it's over with," she said after the game. "I just wanted to stay in the flow of the game, and when it happened, I was happy."

Appropriately, it was Lobo who was UConn's best player against Virginia Tech. She had 17 points, 11 rebounds, eight assists and five blocked shots. Lobo just missed a triple-double and single-handedly equaled the Hokies' assist total. UConn's ball movement, particularly among its front-line players, was impressive. Some of Lobo's prettiest passes came when Virginia Tech double-teamed her down low and she passed to Wolters.

The spirited, seasonlong competition between Rizzotti and freshman Nykesha Sales for UConn's single-season steals record was heightened when Sales got five steals, several of them spectacular. After the game, Sales took the lead with a school-best 92, while Rizzotti stood at 90.

Rebecca Lobo, left, and Nykesha Sales congratulate Jamelle Elliott after Elliott scored her 1,000th point against Virginia Tech. Missy Rose and Pam Webber, far right, join the crowd.

SHERRY PETERS PHOTO

The second-round victory was more impressive than the first because the margin of victory was 46 — even with some of the bench players getting big minutes: Kim Better (16), Kelley Hunt (nine) and Missy Rose (eight).

The Huskies were 31-0 and still winning games by 35. Would the East Regional semifinals and final at Gampel Pavilion March 23 and 25 offer better competition? Alabama, Louisiana Tech and Virginia would be on hand. The prize: a trip to Minneapolis and the Final Four.

Two hours after the game, Auriemma paced in the empty corridor outside the locker room. The games against Maine and Virginia Tech had been almost too easy.

"I mean, I know we're good," Auriemma said. "But are we really that good?

"I guess," he said after a long pause, "we'll find out next week." ■

As Chapter Nine ends:
UConn is 31-0, in the NCAA East Regional semifinals and ranked No. 1.

*"I mean,
I know
we're good.
But are
we really
that good?
I guess
we'll find out
next week."*

• UConn coach
Geno Auriemma

Geno Auriemma
shows Nykesha Sales
where a second-round
victory can take UConn:
to 31-0 and
the semifinals
of the East Regional.

SHERRY PETERS PHOTO

■ CHAPTER TEN

Nothing Rizzotti can't fix

NCAA
East Regional
Semifinals & final
(Gampel Pavilion,
Storrs)

March 23
UConn 87
Alabama 56

March 25
UConn 67
Virginia 63

(Box scores,
Page 140)

The point guard is the pulse of a basketball team, the one who controls the game's tempo and dictates who gets the ball — and when.

Like so many coaches, UConn coach Geno Auriemma was a point guard. He was intuitive, combative and aggressive. He recognized those qualities in Jennifer Rizzotti, which is why he recruited her so hard. More than any player past or present, Auriemma feels, the 5-foot-5 junior from New Fairfield matches his level of intensity.

Sometimes, you can see it in her eyes.

"Every time we play somebody really good," Auriemma said.

Heading into the East Regional semifinals, UConn had faced three critical tests and Rizzotti answered

every time. Against top-ranked Tennessee Jan. 16, she scored 17 points and had a game-high five steals. Twelve days later at Kansas, Rizzotti scored 21 points — 16 in the second half, including nine in a row — to help beat the Jayhawks. Three days after that, when UConn trailed Providence by 11 in the first half, Rizzotti responded with a game-high 19 points.

And so it was March 23 at Gampel Pavilion against Alabama, the No. 4 seed in the region. The Crimson Tide, a combination of muscle and athleticism, used three players to control 6-7 center Kara Wolters and 6-4 forward Rebecca Lobo. It was 13-all 4 minutes, 24 seconds into the game. Rizzotti had scored all but one of UConn's points.

UConn eventually wiped out an 18-15 deficit, took a 26-point lead to the locker room and won, 87-56. But without Rizzotti's early effort, it might have been different. The shortest player on the floor finished with 24 points, eight rebounds, seven assists and two steals.

"That's a question people have continually asked us, how would we play without the

lead?" Lobo said. "What you have to do is get the ball in Jen Rizzotti's hands."

Niesa Johnson, Alabama's first-team All-America guard, was impressed. "We tried to worry about Alabama basketball," she said. "And unfortunately, we should have worried more about UConn basketball. Rizzotti carried them. She made the big

Rebecca Lobo, far left, appreciates the effort of Jamelle Elliott (33) – 12 points in 26 minutes – against Virginia despite foul trouble.

Above, Jamelle Elliott, right, and Rebecca Lobo were on shaky ground against Jenny Boucek, center, and Virginia until a second-half stand.

PAULA BRONSTEIN AND BRAD CLIFT PHOTOS

Jamelle Elliott (33)
doesn't let
a little numbers
problem stop her
against Virginia's
Jenny Boucek,
Wendy Palmer and
Jeffra Gausepohl,
right.

Things go UConn's
way for the
33rd consecutive
time after
Nykesha Sales,
far right,
keeps Virginia
from inbounding
in the final minute.

BRAD CLIFT PHOTOS

plays, and I think she gave them the momentum."

Jamelle Elliott, UConn's junior forward, had another forceful game (15 points and 14 rebounds) and Lobo added 19 points, six rebounds and three blocked shots. The one concern was Wolters, who left the game in the second half with a mild concussion.

The Huskies (32-0) faced Virginia in the East Regional final. The Cavaliers had squeezed past Louisiana Tech in the other semifinal, winning 63-62 on a last-second, court-length dash by guard Tora Suber.

There was history between Virginia and UConn:

• The 1991 national semifinals ended in a 61-55 Virginia victory over UConn. Two of the opposing players, Virginia's Tonya Cardoza and UConn's Meghan Pattyson, were now Auriemma assistants.

• Auriemma had spent four seasons as the assistant to Virginia coach Debbie Ryan.

Before the game, Ryan said her team must achieve three goals to win: 1) rebound with UConn; 2) play sound defense; and 3) stay

with UConn offensively and keep the game in the 60s or 70s. And that's only what Virginia did Saturday morning, March 25, in a game on ESPN.

With Lobo and senior guard Pam Webber playing their last game at Gampel, the Huskies raced to a familiar early lead — it

was 29-10 at the 10-minute mark — and seemed destined to win by their usual 35-point average.

"You can't play any better than we did in the first 10 minutes," Auriemma said. "You can't play any worse than we did in the second 10 minutes."

Six minutes later, Virginia was somehow leading, 34-33. The Cavaliers scored on 13 consecutive possessions and led 44-37 at the half — a first against UConn.

How did they do it? Virginia's All-America Wendy Palmer, a 6-2 forward, 6-6 center Jeffra Gausepohl and 6-1 forward Amy Lofstedt rotated on Lobo and Wolters, with great success. All three were extremely mobile, which explained why Wolters and Elliott went to the locker room with three fouls.

Slowly, UConn climbed back into the game. A left-handed layup by Lobo made it 51-all 9:53 into the second half. But the price UConn paid for its comeback was steep; with 8:07 left, Elliott, Wolters and Rizzotti were all playing with four fouls, one away from fouling out.

And yet, with that narrow margin for error, all three players were key in the final minutes. Back-to-back baskets by freshman Nykesha Sales — the second a careening, fastbreak layup after a strip of Suber — gave UConn a seemingly comfortable 66-57 lead with 4:42 left.

Jennifer Rizzotti, far left, scored 12 of UConn's first 13 points vs. Alabama. Carla Berube appreciates a teammate who is so together.

Carla Berube helps UConn end up ahead of Virginia in the run for a spot in the Final Four, with six points and four assists.

PAULA BRONSTEIN
AND
BRAD CLIFT PHOTOS

Far right, the e
of Amy Lof
and Virg
fell short aga
Kara Wo
(18 points, five blo
and the Husk

After a sca
Geno Auriemma a
his team recover
had a vict
in hand and we
two victories fro
a national championshi

PAULA BRONSTEI
AN
BRAD CLIFT PHOTO

But Virginia came back. UConn was leading 66-63 with 2:05 left when the Huskies' heart surfaced. It was a single-possession game, but:

• Wolters blocked a shot by Palmer.

• Lobo rejected guard Jenny Boucek.

• UConn's dizzying defense prevented Virginia from inbounding in the required five seconds.

• Elliott, fouled by Lofstedt with 18 seconds left, hit a free throw for the final score, 67-63.

And then, the roar of the Gampel crowd was so loud, you could feel it in your chest. Elliott, the only Husky who hadn't lost her composure all game, started to cry. She fell to the court and was buried by her teammates.

They were 33-0 and they were going to Minneapolis.

Rizzotti (13 points, eight rebounds, four assists, two steals), Wolters (18 points, five rebounds, five blocks) and Lobo

From left, a seasonlong
run carries Missy Rose,
Kim Better, Jennifer Rizzotti
(21), Kelley Hunt and
Pam Webber (back)
to the Final Four.

PAULA BRONSTEIN PHOTO

(eight points, six rebounds, six blocks) made the All-Tournament team. But when it was announced that Rizzotti had been voted the outstanding player, she turned to Elliott and shouted, "You deserve it."

An hour later, after Lobo and Webber had kissed the on-court Husky logo and snipped the last strands of the net, Auriemma closed his eyes and leaned against a wall. He seemed more relieved than happy.

"The last two days were very, very different," he said. "The fear creeps in. You worry, 'What happens if this happens? What if that happens?'

"But it's over. We won. We're going to Minneapolis." ■

As Chapter Ten ends:
UConn is 33-0, the NCAA East Regional champion, headed for the Final Four and ranked No. 1.

"The last two days were very, very different. The fear creeps in.
You worry, 'What happens if this happens? What if that happens?'
But it's over. We won. We're going to Minneapolis."

• UConn coach Geno Auriemma

Having cut down the net after beating Virginia, Pam Webber, left, and Rebecca Lobo,
part of the team's fiber, head to Minneapolis.

PAULA BRONSTEIN PHOTO

CHAPTER ELEVEN

They get it done

NCAA Final Four
(Minneapolis)

April 1
UConn 87
Stanford 60

April 2
UConn 70
Tennessee 64

*(Box scores,
Pages 140-141)*

eno Auriemma stood just off the court at the Target Center, looked around at the sellout crowd of 18,038 and said, "We're here."

The UConn coach smiled.

"I just wanted this team to get here," he said, "because they deserved it. From here on in, there's no pressure because we made it to Minneapolis."

He rubbed his hands together and headed for the Huskies' locker room. In a few minutes, they would face Stanford in the NCAA Tournament semifinals on Saturday, April 1.

No pressure? Only in Auriemma's mind.

Thirty-three times they had laced up their high-top sneakers.

Thirty-three times they had taken the court.

Thirty-three times they had won.

And then, it happened again. UConn defeated Stanford with breathtaking ease, 87-60.

Definitive? It was the most one-sided Final Four game in the 14-year history of the tournament. After 11 minutes, it was essentially over.

Center Kara Wolters finished with a game-high 31 points and added nine rebounds and two blocked shots. Forward Jamelle Elliott had 21 points and six rebounds. All-America forward Rebecca Lobo played like the nation's best player, producing this well-rounded line: 17 points, nine rebounds, three assists, three steals and two blocks.

After the game, Auriemma hugged his son Michael, 6, as he answered questions from the media. He was trying his best to savor the most important victory in the history of the program.

"I wish we didn't have to play tomorrow," he said. "I wish we could just get on a flight back to Connecticut and enjoy this one for a long time.

"But if you're going to try to get into the history books, like we are tomorrow, I guess you've got to get up and play."

And so the Huskies stood a single victory from a perfect season. The only women's team to do it previously was Texas in 1985-86. And UConn was in position to go the 34-0 Longhorns one better.

"Kind of scary, really," Elliott said. "We have a chance to do something that's only been done once. We've tried not to talk about it, tried not to think about it, but now it's right there staring us in the face.

"When you start the season, you

Far left, it may be the middle of UConn's 34th consecutive victory but Geno Auriemma still has a few pointers for Kara Wolters. Wolters led UConn with 31 points against Stanford.

Left, Geno Auriemma and Jennifer Rizzotti take some time to get focused during a timeout in the first half of the Tennessee game.

BRAD CLIFT
AND
PAULA BRONSTEIN
PHOTOS

Rebecca Lobo and UConn were off the ground quickly against Stanford and had a record margin of victory for a women's Final Four game.

Far right: With Rebecca Lobo and the Huskies in command, Vanessa Nygaard and Stanford found their pursuit of UConn futile.

BRAD CLIFT PHOTOS

can't imagine being undefeated the whole way. It's hard to believe, but we can make it happen."

All week long, Auriemma said he didn't want to stumble into history like Forrest Gump. All week long, he talked about winning with style.

Now, he had a chance to do both. For Tennessee had earned its way to the final by beating Georgia, 73-51.

The championship game was a rematch of the game that defined the season, when the two highest-ranked teams met Jan. 16 at Gampel Pavilion. In that afternoon game, UConn took the No. 1 ranking from Tennessee with a 77-66 victory.

The prevailing postgame question in Minneapolis: How would that distant result manifest itself Sunday?

As Auriemma put it, "Which would you rather

have — our confidence or their hunger to want to hand it right back to us?"

Tennessee coach Pat Summitt, who had watched the UConn-Stanford game with a trace of a scowl, did her best to sound enthusiastic.

"Well, all you fans, all you people in the media, you got the game you wanted," she said. "Let's just hope they can throw the ball up and we can play a great game."

Auriemma, who had raged on the sidelines several times in the Stanford game, was oddly composed for the Tennessee game. There was only one exception.

There were 3 minutes, 38 seconds left in the first half and Tennessee led, 31-25.

During a timeout, Auriemma slammed the floor with his hands.

"This is it!

"This is it!"

Two of Auriemma's All-Americans — Lobo and Jennifer Rizzotti — already had three fouls. Wolters had two. Meanwhile, Tennessee was trying to run away with the game.

"He was positive. He kept telling us that good things were going to happen," freshman Nykesha Sales said. "He said if we could just hang in there and keep it close, good things would happen. And they did."

The Huskies left the court at halftime trailing 38-32, a reasonable margin considering Lobo sat on the bench the last 12 minutes. She was called for three fouls in 94 seconds.

How important was Lobo to the Huskies? While she was in the game, they made 7 of 9 shots. With Lobo out, they missed 13 of 18.

With UConn struggling to get back in the game in the second half, Lobo wanted the ball. She demanded it.

"We want her to want the ball," Rizzotti said. "We want her to make

the game-winning shot. We want her to win the game for us. That's what she's supposed to do."

Tennessee was leading 52-46 with 11:32 left when Lobo made a post move and got an easy layup. After a steal and a pass by Elliott, Lobo scored again, this time on a driving layup. With 9:03 left, Lobo hit an 18-foot jump shot from the left baseline. At 7:40, she scored again from the left wing.

Five shots, four baskets. Eight of UConn's nine points. UConn trailed, 58-55.

"I don't know if that was the turning point," Lobo said. "I just felt really confident. I felt I could take the game in my own hands. That's a great feeling to not feel helpless — because sometimes you do."

A Rizzotti steal and layup cut Tennessee's lead to 58-57 with 7:06 left. Elliott's free throws with 5:44 to go gave UConn its first lead, 59-58, since 8:38 remaining in the first half. With a three-point play, Tiffani

Above, associate head coach Chris Dailey, third from right, and assistants Meghan Pattyson, second from right and Tonya Cardoza, right, have helped Geno Auriemma's program stand apart.

At left, after making one of her three steals against Tennessee, Jennifer Rizzotti has her eye on two more points for UConn. This same moment during the Huskies' victory is framed on the cover of the April 10 edition of Sports Illustrated.

BRAD CLIFT PHOTOS

Above, from left, Sarah Northway,
Jill Gelfenbien, Brenda Marquis and Kelley Hunt
stand behind UConn, lending support from the bench.
Seated, from left, Missy Rose, Kim Better,
Pam Webber and Carla Berube.

Right, from left, Kelley Hunt, Missy Rose,
Kim Better and Pam Webber leave no doubt
the national champion is UConn.

PAULA BRONSTEIN AND
BRAD CLIFT PHOTOS

Johnson gave the Vols back
the lead, 61-59. Elliott's layup
tied it at 61 with 2:17 left.

Rizzotti then produced the
most memorable moment of
the game. She took a long
rebound and sprinted the
length of the court. Her
Tennessee counterpart,
Michelle Marciniak, was the
only one between her and the
basket. Rizzotti spun
Marciniak with a cross-over
dribble and laid the ball in
left-handed. UConn led 63-61
with 1:51 left.

Then, with 47.5 seconds
left, Rizzotti saved a
bad pass from Lobo
and was fouled by All-
American Nikki McCray. She
made both shots to give
UConn a 65-61 lead it never
lost.

Lobo closed the game with
two epic rebounds and three
free throws and UConn won,
70-64.

And when the buzzer
sounded, Lobo lifted both her

CHAPTER FIVE

After UConn's 35th victory,
Rebecca Lobo, took time to say a prayer
for the accomplishments of a team
so many followed religiously.

BRAD CLIFT PHOTO

long arms and looped around the court, before coming to rest in front of Elliott. They hugged, then jumped into the pile with all their teammates.

They were 35-0. They were perfect.

There have been nine undefeated NCAA champions in the history of men's and women's Division I basketball, but UConn won more games than any other.

Lobo led all players with 17 points and added eight rebounds.

"She made huge plays," Summitt said later. "She made herself hard to guard and got herself jumpers. She beat us one-on-one."

Appropriately, four of the five UConn players who scored in double figures — Lobo, Rizzotti (15), Elliott (13) and Wolters (10) — were named to the Final Four All-Tournament team, another record.

In the end, the totals for the six NCAA Tournament games underlined the team's symmetry:

Wolters scored the most points (108), Elliott had the most rebounds (47), Lobo had the most blocked shots (22), Rizzotti had the most assists (27) and Sales had the most steals (17). Those steals gave Sales, the fifth double-figure scorer (10) in the final, the single-season school record (102), four ahead of Rizzotti.

After the game, Lobo and starting guard Pam Webber, roommates for four years, held the championship trophy aloft. Auriemma was carried off the floor on the shoulders of Lobo and Wolters. After all the tears, embraces and interviews, Auriemma closed his eyes and sighed.

"This," he said, "is the way the story is supposed to end." ■

As Chapter Eleven ends:
UConn is 35-0, ranked No. 1, and national champion.

Undefeated NCAA championship teams

Women

- **1995**
  UConn 35-0
- **1986**
  Texas 34-0

Men

- **1957**
  North Carolina 32-0
- **1976**
  Indiana 32-0
- **1964**
  UCLA 30-0
- **1967**
  UCLA 30-0
- **1972**
  UCLA 30-0
- **1973**
  UCLA 30-0
- **1957**
  San Francisco 29-0

From left,
Carla Berube,
Missy Rose,
Kara Wolters,
Rebecca Lobo,
Nykesha Sales,
Brenda Marquis
(background) and
Jennifer Rizzotti
show their
support for
Geno Auriemma
after beating
Tennessee.

BRAD CLIFT PHOTO

Along championship lines: from left, Nykesha Sales, Jamelle Elliott, Kara Wolters (back), Pam Webber, Rebecca Lobo, Kim Better, Carla Berube (back), Jennifer Rizzotti, Kelley Hunt (back) and Jill Gelfenbien.

■ CHAPTER TWELVE

Statistics, records, awards

Exhibition game 1
Nov. 10, 1994
UConn 61, AIA 58

Athletes in Action

Player	M	FG	FT	RB	A	PF	T
Konerza	24	0-1	1-4	3	4	2	1
Porter	28	7-12	2-2	3	1	2	16
Gillingham	29	3-7	3-4	6	1	1	9
Evans	34	3-8	0-0	3	3	2	7
Ware	30	4-4	0-0	3	4	2	8
Pontius	21	3-12	2-3	2	0	3	8
Salamone	16	0-1	4-4	2	2	1	4
Donovan	12	2-5	0-0	0	1	2	4
Link	6	0-0	1-2	0	0	2	1
Totals	200	22-50	13-19	31	16	17	58

Three-point goals: 1-4 (Evans 1-2, Salamone 0-1, Donovan 0-1). **FG pct.:** 44.0; **FT pct.:** 68.4. **Team rebounds:** 9. **TO:** 22 (Evans 6, Gillingham 5, Porter 4, Salamone 3, Konerza 2, Ware, Donovan). **Blocks:** 2 (Gillingham 2). **Steals:** 15 (Ware 5, Salamone 3, Evans 3, Porter, Konerza, Gillingham, Pontius).

Connecticut

Player	M	FG	FT	RB	A	PF	T
Elliott	33	6-10	1-3	4	3	4	14
Lobo	27	3-7	0-1	6	3	4	6
Wolters	34	9-13	0-1	9	2	4	18
Rizzotti	35	3-9	2-3	2	6	3	8
Webber	20	0-2	0-0	3	0	2	0
Better	25	2-6	0-0	2	5	1	4
Sales	25	3-8	3-4	2	1	2	11
Hunt	1	0-0	0-0	1	0	0	0
Totals	200	26-55	6-12	33	20	20	61

Three-point goals: 3-16 (Sales 2-5, Elliott 1-1, Better 0-2, Webber 0-2, Lobo 0-1, Rizzotti 0-5). **FG pct.:** 47.3 **FT pct.:** 50.0. **Team rebounds:** 4. **TO:** 24 (Rizzotti 7, Lobo 5, Elliott 4, Webber 3, Sales 2, Better, Hunt, Wolters). **Blocks:** 6 (Lobo 4, Wolters 2). **Steals:** 15 (Sales 4, Better 3, Webber 3, Rizzotti 2, Elliott 2, Lobo).

Halftime — AIA, 28-27
Officials — Frank Geiselman, Daryl Hardcastle
Attendance — 5,937 at Gampel Pavilion, Storrs

Exhibition game 2
Nov. 16
UConn 100, Rossianka 77

Rossianka (Moscow)

Player	M	FG	FT	RB	A	PF	T
Jeldacheva	26	1-10	2-2	1	2	5	5
Kouzntsva	16	1-7	0-0	2	0	3	2
Astalieva	35	5-14	0-0	8	0	3	11
Masalova	39	12-24	0-0	2	3	5	33
Avibova	36	1-6	4-6	9	3	4	6
Vazchlna,N	28	6-12	6-7	5	3	2	18
Kharlanova	5	0-0	0-0	0	0	2	0
Vesselkina	7	0-1	0-0	0	0	1	0
Vazchlna,A	5	0-0	0-0	1	0	1	0
Rogozina	3	1-4	0-0	2	0	1	2
Totals	200	27-78	12-15	37	11	27	77

Three-point goals: 11-30 (Masalova 9-19, Jeldacheva 1-7, Astalieva 1-3, Avibova 0-1). **FG pct.:** 34.6; **FT pct.:** 80.0. **Team rebounds:** 7. **TO:** 12 (Jeldacheva 4, Astalieva 3, VazouchilinaN 2, Astalieva, Avibova, Vazouchilina,A). **Blocks:** 1 (Astalieva). **Steals:** 4 (Kharlanova 2, Avibova, Jeldacheva). **Fouled out:** Jeldacheva, Masalova

Connecticut

Player	M	FG	FT	RB	A	PF	T
Elliott	33	4-8	4-4	7	2	4	12
Lobo	30	6-11	6-6	10	4	2	19
Wolters	22	11-15	3-3	5	1	3	25
Better	26	2-5	3-5	2	3	0	7
Webber	36	3-5	4-5	4	7	2	10
Sales	22	4-10	7-7	2	2	1	15
Rose	12	1-3	0-0	1	0	2	2
Hunt	12	2-3	0-0	6	0	1	4
Marquis	7	2-2	2-4	1	0	0	6
Totals	200	35-62	29-34	45	19	15	100

Three-point goals: 1-6 (Lobo 1-3, Sales 0-2, Webber 0-1). **FG pct.:** 56.5; **FT pct.:** 85.3. **Team rebounds:** 7. **TO:** 12 (Elliott 4, Lobo 2, Webber 2, Sales 2, Hunt 2). **Blocks:** 6 (Elliott 2, Lobo 2, Wolters, Marquis). **Steals:** 8 (Sales 3, Better 2, Elliott, Lobo, Hunt).

Halftime — UConn, 49-39
Officials — Joanne Aldrich, Larry Savo
Attendance — 4,868 at Gampel Pavilion, Storrs

Game 1
Nov. 26
Hartford Courant Classic
UConn 107, Morgan St. 27

Morgan State

Player	M	FG	FT	RB	A	PF	T
Saffold	29	0-7	0-0	4	0	1	0
Wimberly	12	0-1	0-0	1	1	1	0
Holman	19	1-5	0-0	2	0	4	2
Warfld, Kla.	32	4-12	0-0	2	0	2	9
Warfld, Kra.	13	0-8	1-2	0	0	5	1
McGriff	13	0-0	0-0	0	0	1	0
Womack	13	1-8	0-0	4	0	3	2
Johnson	20	2-12	0-0	4	0	3	4
Muhammd	17	1-9	0-0	2	1	2	2
Dugan	22	3-3	1-2	2	0	4	7
Hall	10	0-1	0-0	1	0	2	0
Totals	200	12-66	2-4	32	2	28	27

Three-point goals: 1-8 (Warfield, Kla. 1-3, Holman 0-2, Saffold 0-2, Muhammad 0-1). **FG pct.:** 18.2; **FT pct.:** 50.0. **Team rebounds:** 10. **TO:** 28. **Blocks:** 4. **Steals:** 6; **Fouled out:** Warfield, Kra.

Connecticut

Player	M	FG	FT	RB	A	PF	T
Elliott	22	3-3	3-6	10	2	2	9
Lobo	25	8-11	2-3	13	7	1	18
Wolters	14	6-6	0-0	5	0	0	12
Rizzotti	16	2-5	2-3	4	6	0	7
Webber	29	2-6	4-4	2	6	1	9
Sales	27	7-13	0-2	8	0	1	15
Better	19	5-8	2-4	3	1	1	13
Rose	17	2-6	4-4	3	0	0	9
Hunt	19	0-4	6-6	7	1	2	6
Marquis	12	3-6	3-4	4	0	1	9
Totals	200	38-68	26-36	65	23	9	107

Three-point goals: 5-10 (Rizzotti 1-3, Webber 1-2, Better 1-2, Rose 1-2, Sales 1-1). **FG pct.:** 55.9; **FT pct.:** 72.2. **Team rebounds:** 6. **TO:** 16. **Blocks:** 9. **Steals:** 15.

Halftime — UConn, 55-11
Officials — Dennis DeMayo, Ike Relacion
Attendance — 5,623 at Gampel Pavilion, Storrs

Game 2
Nov. 27
Hartford Courant Classic
UConn 92, Rhode Island 59

Rhode Island

Player	M	FG	FT	RB	A	PF	T
Byrd	34	5-15	0-0	4	2	2	11
King	32	6-17	0-2	5	0	1	14
Bright	32	4-15	2-2	5	0	2	10
Smith	26	2-7	0-0	2	5	3	5
Giroux	26	3-9	0-0	3	1	4	8
Williams	17	1-3	0-0	2	1	1	3
Fuller	18	1-11	0-0	4	0	3	2
Nelson	14	2-5	2-2	3	2	1	6
Smith	1	0-0	0-0	0	0	0	0
Totals	200	24-82	4-6	37	11	17	59

Three-point goals: 7-19 (King 2-5, Giroux 2-6, Byrd 1-2, Williams 1-2, Smith 1-3, Bright 0-1). FG pct.: 29.3; FT pct.: 66.7. Team rebounds: 9. TO: 20. Blocks: 3. Steals: 6.

Connecticut

Player	M	FG	FT	RB	A	PF	T
Elliott	17	4-6	0-0	5	1	5	9
Lobo	31	10-18	0-0	12	7	1	21
Wolters	25	9-13	0-0	7	0	1	18
Rizzotti	23	3-7	2-4	3	1	2	9
Webber	35	1-3	2-2	4	5	1	4
Sales	23	5-7	2-2	5	3	0	14
Better	21	3-8	2-4	5	4	2	8
Hunt	8	1-3	0-0	3	0	0	2
Rose	9	0-2	1-1	2	0	1	1
Marquis	8	3-6	0-0	3	0	0	6
Totals	200	39-73	9-13	57	21	13	92

Three-point goals: 5-10 (Sales 2-3, Elliott 1-1, Lobo 1-1, Rizzotti 1-2, Better 0-2, Webber 0-1). FG pct.: 53.4; FT pct.: 69.2. Team rebounds: 8. TO: 24. Blocks: 15. Steals: 11; Fouled out: Elliott. Technical foul: Better.

Halftime — UConn, 42-28
Officials — Dennis DeMayo, Tony Fountain
Attendance — 5,782 at Gampel Pavilion, Storrs

Game 3
Dec. 4
UConn 80
Villanova 42

Villanova

Player	M	FG	FT	RB	A	PF	T
Snell	15	2-4	0-0	1	1	1	4
Dillon	25	4-13	1-1	6	0	1	9
Rosenthal	15	0-5	1-2	9	0	2	1
Glenning	18	0-7	0-0	3	0	4	0
Thornton	27	1-9	2-3	0	1	3	5
Maga	17	0-7	0-0	4	1	1	0
Baglio	20	1-4	0-0	2	4	3	2
Higgins	17	5-9	0-0	1	0	1	11
Keffer	16	0-2	1-2	1	0	0	1
Beisel	14	2-7	0-0	1	2	1	5
Bradshaw	7	0-4	1-2	0	1	2	1
Hightower	6	1-2	0-0	0	0	1	2
Gaziano	3	0-0	1-2	0	0	0	1
Totals	200	16-73	7-12	28	10	21	42

Three-point goals: 3-19 (Thornton 1-6, Baglio 0-2, Glenning 0-5, Higgins 1-3, Keffer 0-2, Beisel 1-1). FG pct.: 21.9; FT pct.: 58.3. Team rebounds: 7. TO: 16. Blocks: 0. Steals: 11.

Connecticut

Player	M	FG	FT	RB	A	PF	T
Elliott	24	4-5	5-7	11	3	2	13
Lobo	29	4-15	1-5	16	3	1	9
Wolters	23	7-14	1-2	5	1	1	15
Rizzotti	26	4-7	3-5	5	3	3	12
Webber	21	1-2	0-0	3	1	0	2
Sales	21	4-6	2-2	2	2	2	11
Better	20	0-2	6-8	4	1	1	6
Berube	16	1-2	0-0	2	1	2	2
Hunt	6	2-3	1-1	0	0	0	5
Rose	6	1-1	0-0	3	1	1	3
Marquis	5	1-1	0-0	2	0	0	2
Gelfenbien	3	0-0	0-0	1	0	1	0
Totals	200	29-58	19-30	61	16	14	80

Three-point goals: 3-6 (Rizzotti 1-2, Lobo 0-1, Sales 1-2, Rose 1-1). FG pct.: 50.0; FT pct.: 63.3. Team rebounds: 7. TO: 20. Blocks: 11. Steals: 10.

Halftime — UConn, 36-19
Officials — Frank Geiselman, Deborah Allen
Attendance — 6,124 at Gampel Pavilion, Storrs

Game 4
Dec. 7
UConn 77, Holy Cross 52

Connecticut

Player	M	FG	FT	RB	A	PF	T
Better	21	1-6	0-0	2	2	3	2
Rose	7	0-4	1-2	0	0	0	1
Rizzotti	19	7-13	0-0	0	1	2	16
Marquis	5	0-1	0-1	2	1	1	0
Berube	18	2-4	0-2	4	1	0	6
Webber	32	1-7	0-0	3	7	3	3
Elliott	29	5-14	7-8	12	3	1	18
Hunt	3	1-1	0-0	0	0	0	2
Gelfenbien	2	0-0	0-0	1	0	0	0
Sales	20	7-10	1-3	3	1	1	15
Lobo	30	3-13	3-5	14	1	2	10
Wolters	14	1-5	2-5	6	0	3	4
Totals	200	28-78	14-26	52	17	16	77

Three-point goals: 7-24, .292 (Better 0-2, Rose 0-4, Rizzotti 2-6, Berube 2-2, Webber 1-7, Elliott 1-1, Sales 0-1, Lobo 1-1). FG pct.: 35.9; FT pct.: 53.8. Team rebounds: 5. TO: 14 (Better, Rizzotti, Marquis, Berube 2, Webber 3, Elliott 3, Hunt 2, Sales). Blocks: 2 (Berube, Lobo). Steals: 16 (Rizzotti 6, Sales 4, Lobo 2, Better, Rose, Marquis, Webber).

Holy Cross

Player	M	FG	FT	RB	A	PF	T
Maney	35	4-11	0-0	3	4	2	8
Lynch	36	4-11	0-0	2	4	1	12
Bostic	2	0-2	0-0	1	0	0	0
Pena	4	0-1	2-2	0	0	0	2
Dietz	27	3-4	1-2	3	2	4	8
Monahan	4	0-1	0-0	0	0	0	0
Gardner	10	0-1	0-0	2	0	2	0
Juda	25	2-4	0-0	6	0	2	4
Courtney	31	1-6	0-4	6	3	4	2
Machut	3	1-1	0-0	0	0	2	2
Porath	2	0-0	0-0	0	0	0	0
Lee	16	6-7	2-3	2	1	3	14
Cotta	2	0-0	0-0	1	0	1	0
Bradley	3	0-0	0-0	1	0	0	0
Totals	200	21-49	5-11	32	14	20	52

Three-point goals: 5-16, .313 (Maney 0-2, Lynch 4-10, Bostic 0-2, Dietz 1-1, Monahan 0-1). FG pct.: 42.9; FT pct.: 45.5. Team rebounds: 5. TO: 27 (Maney 2, Lynch 7, Dietz 3, Monahan, Gardner 2, Juda 3, Courtney 4, Machut, Lee 3). Blocks: 6 (Juda 2, Courtney 4, Lee). Steals: 5 (Maney 2, Bostic, Dietz, Machut).

Halftime — UConn, 34-21
Officials — Jack Riordan, Larry Sabo
Attendance — 2,583 at Hart Center, Worcester

Game 5
Dec. 10
UConn 98
N.C. State 75

Connecticut

Player	M	FG	FT	RB	A	PF	T
Rizzotti	27	6-13	0-0	3	2	4	14
Webber	26	2-3	1-2	4	2	2	7
Elliott	32	8-12	3-4	7	3	3	21
Lobo	31	8-11	7-8	9	6	2	24
Wolters	15	4-6	0-2	3	1	5	8
Better	16	0-1	1-2	2	2	2	1
Rose	5	0-0	0-0	0	0	1	0
Marquis	3	1-1	0-0	0	0	0	2
Berube	15	3-6	5-6	3	0	0	11
Hunt	2	0-0	0-0	0	0	0	0
Gelfenbien	2	0-0	0-0	0	0	0	0
Sales	26	3-6	2-3	8	2	4	10
Totals	200	35-59	19-27	41	25	23	98

Three-point goals: 9-11, .818 (Rizzotti 2-4, Webber 2-2, Elliott 2-2, Sales 2-2, Lobo 1-1). **FG pct.:** 59.3; **FT pct.:** 70.4. **Team rebounds:** 2. **TO:** 18 (Elliott 5, Sales 3, Rizzotti 2, Lobo 2, Wolters 2, Rose, Marquis, Berube, Hunt). **Blocks:** 2 (Lobo, Sales). **Steals:** 6 (Rizzotti 2, Elliott, Lobo, Sales). **Fouled out:** Wolters

North Carolina State

Player	M	FG	FT	RB	A	PF	T
Gibson	32	5-16	0-0	4	2	2	12
Howard	37	6-8	5-6	1	1	1	21
Webb	31	4-16	2-4	7	10	4	10
Kreul	26	2-7	4-4	2	2	4	8
Floyd	24	1-4	0-0	5	4	5	2
Poteat	3	0-0	0-0	0	0	0	0
Davis	7	1-1	2-2	0	0	2	4
Young	15	2-3	0-0	0	0	0	6
Melvin	25	5-7	2-3	4	2	3	12
Totals	200	26-62	15-19	25	21	21	75

Three-point goals: 8-23, .348 (Gibson 2-10, Howard 4-4, Webb 0-6, Kreul 0-1, Young 2-2). **FG pct.:** 41.9; **FT pct.:** 78.9. **Team rebounds:** 2. **TO:** 20 (Webb 8, Kreul 3, Melvin 3, Gibson 2, Davis 2, Howard, Floyd). **Blocks:** 3 (Webb, Floyd, Melvin). **Steals:** 3 (Webb 2, Kreul). **Fouled out:** Floyd

Halftime — UConn, 45-36.
Officials — D. Cloud, W. Franklin, R. Frankoff.
Attendance — 1,066 at Reynolds Coliseum, Raleigh, N.C.

Game 6
Dec. 23
UConn 101
Iona 42

Iona

Player	M	FG	FT	RB	A	PF	T
Gore	26	1-7	0-0	2	0	2	2
Zimmermn	32	1-4	0-0	3	2	2	2
Tacopina	21	5-14	0-0	0	0	3	10
Seltzer	29	2-12	0-0	1	2	1	6
Granes	22	0-3	0-0	1	2	1	0
Radday	28	3-11	0-0	2	1	1	9
Roberts	18	2-7	2-2	4	0	1	6
Malsbendn	17	2-5	1-5	2	1	2	5
Hazen	7	1-1	0-0	3	0	2	0
Totals	200	17-64	3-7	21	8	13	42

Three-point goals: 5-17 (Radday 3-9, Seltzer 2-5, Gore 0-1, Roberts 0-1, Malsbenden 0-1). **FG pct.:** 26.7; **FT pct.:** 42.9. **Team rebounds:** 3. **TO:** 20. **Steals:** 8 (Radday 4). **Blocks:** 2 (Malsbenden 2).

Connecticut

Player	M	FG	FT	RB	A	PF	T
Elliott	20	3-5	4-4	9	3	0	10
Lobo	19	11-11	3-4	9	3	0	25
Wolters	15	6-7	0-0	2	0	0	12
Rizzotti	16	1-4	0-0	2	6	0	3
Webber	19	3-4	0-0	3	6	1	7
Better	28	1-5	3-4	6	7	2	5
Sales	13	5-9	0-0	8	1	1	10
Berube	13	3-6	2-2	5	3	1	8
Rose	23	3-5	0-0	0	1	1	7
Marquis	14	5-5	0-0	2	0	1	10
Hunt	14	1-6	0-0	2	2	0	2
Gelfenbien	6	1-2	0-0	3	0	1	2
Totals	200	43-69	12-14	56	32	8	101

Three-point goals: 3-10 (Rizzotti 1-2, Webber 1-2, Rose 1-2, Sales 0-1, Berube 0-1, Better 0-2). **FG pct.:** 62.3; **FT pct.:** 85.7. **Team rebounds:** 5. **TO:** 17. **Steals:** 12 (Better 3, Rose 3). **Blocks:** 5 (Lobo 4).

Halftime — UConn, 55-16.
Officials — Frank Geiselman, Joanne Aldrich.
Attendance — 6,725 at Gampel Pavilion, Storrs

Game 7
Dec. 28
UConn 99
California 52

California

Player	M	FG	FT	RB	A	PF	T
Barrett	4	0-1	0-0	2	0	0	0
Tatum	25	3-12	0-2	3	0	1	8
Snijder	35	2-8	1-2	6	0	2	5
Lear	38	5-11	0-2	1	5	1	11
Sokolwska	35	4-14	0-0	3	3	3	8
Czepiec	23	5-9	1-2	3	1	4	14
Folsom	9	0-2	0-0	0	0	1	0
Oldenbrger	16	3-6	0-0	2	0	2	6
Tamony	6	0-1	0-0	0	0	0	0
Dmitrieva	4	0-0	0-0	0	0	1	0
Rizzo	3	0-0	0-0	0	0	1	0
Scotty	2	0-0	0-0	0	0	0	0
Totals	200	22-64	2-8	26	9	16	52

Three-point goals: 6-15 (Tatum 2-5, Lear 1-2, Sokolowska 0-1, Czepiec 3-6, Tamony 0-1). **FG pct.:** 34.4; **FT pct.:** 25.0. **Team rebounds:** 6. **TO:** 24 (Sokolowska 11, Tatum 4, Snijder 3, Czepiec 3, Lear, Folsom, Oldenburger). **Blocks:** 2 (Snijder, Dmitrieva). **Steals:** 10 (Sokolowska 4, Lear 3, Tatum 2, Czepiec).

Connecticut

Player	M	FG	FT	RB	A	PF	T
Elliott	23	6-9	2-2	5	4	4	14
Lobo	24	8-17	1-2	16	5	1	18
Wolters	23	10-15	0-0	9	4	1	20
Rizzotti	24	4-8	0-0	1	6	2	9
Webber	28	3-5	0-1	5	6	2	6
Sales	12	4-5	3-4	2	1	1	12
Better	17	2-5	3-3	1	4	1	7
Berube	18	4-7	0-1	4	0	0	8
Rose	17	1-1	0-0	3	0	3	2
Hunt	6	0-2	2-2	4	1	0	2
Marquis	5	0-1	1-2	2	0	1	1
Gelfenbien	3	0-0	0-0	0	0	0	0
Totals	200	42-75	12-17	55	31	16	99

Three-point goals: 3-9 (Lobo 1-2, Rizzotti 1-3, Webber 0-1, Sales 1-2, Better 0-1). **FG pct.:** 56.0; **FT pct.:** 70.6. **Team rebounds:** 3. **TO:** 18 (Berube 5, Webber 4, Elliott 3, Better 2, Lobo, Sales, Hunt, Marquis). **Blocks:** 9 (Wolters 5, Lobo 2, Webber, Sales). **Steals:** 14 (Rizzotti 4, Better 3, Lobo 2, Wolters, Webber, Berube, Rose, Hunt).

Halftime — UConn, 55-13.
Officials — Pat Sullivan, Larry Savo.
Attendance — 8,241 at Gampel Pavilion, Storrs

Game 8
Jan. 2, 1995
UConn 100
Pittsburgh 67

Pittsburgh

Player	M	FG	FT	RB	A	PF	T
Joyce	34	5-12	2-4	2	2	1	15
Thompson	31	3-11	2-4	6	0	1	8
Howard	22	6-21	1-2	5	0	3	13
Petho	21	5-10	1-2	5	2	2	11
Morton	29	3-12	0-1	5	11	3	6
Miller	11	0-4	0-0	0	1	1	0
Woods	11	1-3	0-0	3	0	0	2
Guzman	11	1-5	0-0	0	0	1	3
Bolfert	12	1-1	0-0	2	0	1	2
Senneca	10	0-3	1-2	1	0	2	1
Fornadel	7	3-4	0-0	3	0	1	6
Warren	1	0-0	0-0	0	0	1	0
Totals	200	28-86	7-15	38	16	17	67

Three-point goals: 4-13, 30.8 (Joyce 3-4, Miller 0-3, Guzman 1-5, Senneca 0-1). **FG pct.:** .326; **FT pct.:** .467. **Team rebounds:** 6. **TO:** 16 (Joyce, Thompson 3, Howard, Petho, Morton 5, Woods 2, Guzman 2, Bolfert). **Blocks:** 1 (Howard). **Steals:** 6 (Joyce, Petho, Morton 3, Woods).

Connecticut

Player	M	FG	FT	RB	A	PF	T
Elliott	19	6-9	2-2	5	3	3	14
Lobo	27	2-6	1-2	8	7	0	5
Wolters	24	7-8	0-0	12	2	1	14
Rizzotti	25	7-9	4-5	2	6	2	22
Webber	24	2-5	1-2	6	4	0	6
Sales	18	5-7	1-3	2	1	2	11
Better	21	5-7	5-5	3	4	4	15
Berube	17	3-7	0-2	6	0	2	6
Rose	12	1-3	0-0	0	1	1	3
Hunt	6	2-2	0-0	0	0	0	4
Marquis	4	0-0	0-0	1	0	1	0
Gelfenbien	3	0-0	0-0	0	0	0	0
Totals	200	40-63	14-21	48	28	16	100

Three-point goals: 6-14, 42.9 (Lobo 0-2, Rizzotti 4-6, Webber 1-3, Sales 0-1, Berube 0-1, Rose 1-1). **FG pct.:** .635; **FT pct.:** .667. **Team rebounds:** 3. **TO:** 22 (Elliott 2, Lobo, Wolters 3, Rizzotti 4, Webber 4, Sales, Better 4, Rose). **Blocks:** 10 (Wolters 5, Lobo 4, Berube). **Steals:** 9 (Lobo 2, Wolters, Rizzotti 3, Webber, Sales, Better).

Halftime — UConn, 53-27
Officials — Jack Riordan, Tom Danaher
Attendance — 7,212 at Gampel Pavilion, Storrs

Game 9
Jan. 5
UConn 103
Georgetown 64

Connecticut

Player	M	FG	FT	RB	A	PF	T
Elliott	28	4-11	3-3	15	3	2	11
Lobo	26	3-6	3-4	9	1	2	9
Wolters	16	4-7	2-2	6	2	3	10
Rizzotti	29	8-13	2-3	3	7	1	21
Webber	27	0-2	6-8	1	5	2	6
Better	15	2-5	2-2	3	3	0	6
Rose	10	2-3	0-0	2	0	0	4
Marquis	3	0-2	0-0	3	0	0	0
Berube	16	6-10	0-1	6	1	2	13
Hunt	5	1-2	0-0	0	0	2	2
Gelfenbien	3	0-0	0-0	0	0	1	0
Sales	22	9-13	2-2	3	0	2	21
Totals	200	39-74	20-25	58	22	17	103

Three-point goals: 5-14 (Rizzotti 3-7, Berube 1-2, Sales 1-2, Lobo 0-1, Weber 0-1, Better 0-1) **FG pct.:** 52.7; **FT pct.:** 80. **Team rebounds:** 7. **TO:** 19 (Elliott 5, Lobo 5, Better 3, Rizzotti 2, Wolters, Webber, Marquis, Hunt). **Blocks:** 2 (Lobo, Wolters). **Steals:** 7 (Rizzotti 3, Lobo 2, Better, Sales).

Georgetown

Player	M	FG	FT	RB	A	PF	T
Hanrahan	28	2-7	0-0	2	1	0	6
Jacobsen	28	4-10	0-0	9	4	2	8
LaForce	17	7-12	0-1	4	0	2	14
Pendrghst	22	3-9	2-2	3	1	2	10
Williams	27	3-10	1-2	3	3	3	7
Gallon	20	3-10	1-2	0	1	3	7
DeShayes	5	0-0	0-0	0	0	0	0
Ahonkhai	25	1-11	3-4	5	0	1	5
Nixon	15	1-6	1-2	4	0	3	3
Staier	10	1-2	2-5	0	0	3	4
Klauson	3	0-2	0-0	0	0	0	0
Totals	200	25-79	10-18	39	10	19	64

Three-point goals: 4-16 (Hanrahan 2-5, Penderghast 2-5, Gallon 0-4, Jacobsen 0-2.) **FG pct.:** 31.6; **FT pct.:** 55.6. **Team rebounds:** 9. **TO:** 17 (Penderghast 5, Gallon 3, Hanrahan 2, LaForce 2, Staier 2, Jacobsen, Ahonkhai, Nixon). **Blocks:** 0. **Steals:** 8 (Penderghast 2, Ahonkhai 2, Nixon 2, Jacobsen, LaForce).

Halftime — UConn, 58-32
Officials — Yvette McKinney, Dennis DeMayo
Attendance — 1,005 at McDonough Arena, Washington

Game 10
Jan. 7
UConn 98, St. John's 64

Connecticut

Player	M	FG	FT	RB	A	PF	T
Elliott	19	5-9	2-2	6	2	4	13
Lobo	30	8-13	6-8	7	2	3	24
Wolters	23	6-9	3-4	9	2	0	15
Rizzotti	23	2-8	2-3	0	4	1	6
Webber	30	0-0	0-1	3	6	2	0
Better	16	3-4	1-1	4	3	3	8
Rose	6	0-0	0-0	0	0	2	0
Marquis	4	2-4	0-1	2	0	0	4
Berube	17	3-6	5-6	10	3	3	11
Hunt	5	0-3	0-1	3	0	1	0
Gelfenbien	4	1-2	0-0	3	0	0	2
Sales	23	5-10	4-4	2	4	0	15
Totals	200	35-68	23-31	54	26	19	98

Three-point goals: 5-10, 50.0 (Lobo 2-2, Better 1-2, Sales 1-2, Elliott 1-1, Rizzotti 0-2, Berube 0-1). **FG pct.:** 51.5; **FT pct.:** 74.2. **Team rebounds:** 5. **TO:** 21 (Webber 4, Elliott 3, Lobo 3, Wolters 3, Berube 3, Sales 2, Rizzotti, Rose, Hunt). **Blocks:** 2 (Wolters 2). **Steals:** 16 (Rizzotti 6, Elliott 2, Better 2, Berube 2, Hunt 2, Sales 2).

St. John's

Player	M	FG	FT	RB	A	PF	T
Collins	25	3-9	1-3	5	2	3	7
Kelly	19	2-9	0-0	3	1	1	5
Crawford	19	1-4	1-2	7	0	3	3
Price	29	6-11	0-0	3	2	5	13
Jackson	31	7-14	0-0	3	3	1	15
DeLorenzo	2	0-1	0-2	0	0	0	0
Lynch	3	0-1	0-0	0	0	0	0
Lattanzio	15	2-4	0-0	3	0	3	4
Schell	13	1-5	2-2	2	1	0	5
Burke	12	2-4	1-2	2	0	3	5
Aponte	12	1-8	0-0	0	1	3	3
Oliver	11	1-5	0-3	5	0	2	2
Crockett	9	1-4	0-0	0	0	2	2
Totals	200	27-79	5-14	43	10	26	64

Three-point goals: 5-17, 29.4 (Grace 1-4, Price 1-2, Jackson 1-2, Schell 1-4, Aponte 1-4, Collins 0-1). **FG pct.:** 34.2; **FT pct.:** 35.7. **Team rebounds:** 10. **TO:** 21 (Jackson 5, Kelly 4, Crawford 4, Collins 2, Lynch, Lattanzio, Schell, Aponte, Oliver, Crockett). **Blocks:** 1 (Crawford). **Steals:** 14 (Price 3, Kelly 2, Lattanzio 2, Collins, Crawford, Jackson, Lynch, Burke, Aponte, Oliver).

Halftime — UConn, 55-25
Officials — Deborah Allen, Larry Savo
Attendance — 872 at Alumni Hall, Jamaica, N.Y.

Game 11
Jan. 11
UConn 104
Providence 50

Providence

Player	M	FG	FT	RB	A	PF	T
Miller	23	0-2	1-2	5	0	5	1
Chatten	37	4-18	3-5	11	0	1	12
Penrod	30	4-7	2-2	4	0	2	10
Cavallo	35	0-12	0-0	1	2	0	0
Walden	33	6-16	5-6	3	2	4	17
Bresnahan	30	3-14	2-2	3	2	4	10
Malone	12	0-2	0-0	1	0	1	0
Totals	200	17-71	13-17	37	6	17	50

Three-point goals: 3-27 (Bresnahan 2-12, Chatten 1-3, Cavallo 0-10, Walden 0-2). **FG pct.:** 23.9; **FT pct.:** 76.5. **Team rebounds:** 9. **TO:** 21 (Walden 8, Chatten 4, Miller, Bresnahan 3, Penrod 2, Cavallo). **Blocks:** 1 (Chatten). **Steals:** 7 (Chatten 4, Penrod, Cavallo, Walden). **Fouled out:** Miller

Connecticut

Player	M	FG	FT	RB	A	PF	T
Elliott	15	3-6	0-0	5	2	2	8
Lobo	22	6-12	2-2	7	3	2	14
Wolters	19	5-9	0-0	14	2	2	10
Rizzotti	13	3-6	2-2	1	2	3	8
Webber	29	3-9	0-0	2	5	3	9
Sales	18	4-10	2-2	9	2	2	10
Berube	21	7-16	4-5	9	4	4	18
Better	25	6-9	3-4	6	1	2	17
Rose	18	1-4	0-1	5	2	0	2
Hunt	7	1-2	2-4	3	1	2	4
Marquis	8	2-5	0-0	3	2	0	4
Gelfenbien	5	0-1	0-0	0	0	0	0
Totals	200	41-89	15-20	70	26	22	104

Three-point goals: 7-17 (Webber 3-5, Elliott 2-2, Better 2-3, Sales 0-2, Berube 0-2, Rose 0-3). **FG pct.:** 46.1; **FT pct.:** 75.0. **Team rebounds:** 6. **TO:** 18 (Lobo 5, Wolters 2, Webber 2, Sales 2, Hunt 2, Elliott, Rizzotti, Better, Rose, Marquis). **Blocks:** 4 (Lobo, Wolters, Better, Marquis). **Steals:** 9 (Sales 3, Better 3, Elliott, Lobo, Berube).

Halftime — UConn, 53-22.
Officials — Jack Plunkett, Ed Meier.
Attendance — 6,010 at Gampel Pavilion, Storrs

Game 12
Jan. 13
UConn 80
Seton Hall 36

Seton Hall

Player	M	FG	FT	RB	A	PF	T
Wynne	29	5-15	1-2	12	0	5	11
Quinney	23	1-9	0-2	2	3	4	2
Johnson	29	5-17	2-2	7	0	2	12
Heins	35	0-6	0-0	7	2	2	0
Walker	24	2-8	0-0	4	2	3	4
Mitchell	11	2-7	0-0	1	0	5	5
Turner	22	0-4	2-2	5	0	1	2
Makarewicz	4	0-2	0-0	0	0	0	0
Nelson	8	0-3	0-3	2	0	0	0
Brookins	11	0-2	0-0	1	0	1	0
Busichio	4	0-2	0-0	0	0	1	0
Totals	200	15-75	5-11	46	7	24	36

Three-point goals: 1-7 (Mitchell 1-3, Walker 0-1, Makarewicz 0-1, Heins 0-2). **FG pct.:** 20.0; **FT pct.:** 45.5. **Team rebounds:** 5. **TO:** 25. **Steals:** 9 (Heins 3). **Blocks:** 7 (Johnson 4). **Fouled out:** Wynne, Mitchell.

Connecticut

Player	M	FG	FT	RB	A	PF	T
Elliott	20	2-4	0-0	3	2	3	5
Lobo	33	4-11	5-8	14	4	1	13
Wolters	25	6-10	0-3	4	0	3	12
Rizzotti	22	5-6	3-4	3	4	3	15
Webber	24	0-2	0-0	6	3	1	0
Sales	23	5-10	5-8	4	3	1	17
Better	19	0-5	5-10	6	2	0	5
Berube	15	2-3	0-1	3	0	2	5
Rose	6	0-1	0-0	0	0	0	0
Hunt	5	0-1	0-2	2	0	1	0
Marquis	4	3-4	0-0	4	0	1	6
Gelfenbien	4	1-2	0-0	1	0	0	2
Totals	200	28-59	18-36	60	18	18	80

Three-point goals: 6-14 (Rizzotti 2-3, Sales 2-3, Berube 1-1, Elliott 1-2, Webber 0-1, Better 0-1, Rose 0-1, Lobo 0-2). **FG pct.:** 47.5; **FT pct.:** 50.0. **Team rebounds:** 10. **TO:** 24. **Steals:** 13 (Sales 5). **Blocks:** 17 (Lobo 9).

Halftime — UConn, 37-16.
Officials — Phyllis Deveney, Bob McEntee.
Attendance — 7,659 at Gampel Pavilion, Storrs

Game 13
Jan. 16
UConn 77
Tennessee 66

Tennessee

Player	M	FG	FT	RB	A	PF	T
McCray	37	2-10	6-10	7	1	2	10
D.Johnson	29	6-13	2-4	8	0	4	14
T.Johnson	32	6-10	2-2	5	0	2	14
Marciniak	30	5-14	0-0	3	4	4	12
Davis	22	4-10	1-2	4	3	5	10
Ward	12	0-2	0-0	4	0	4	0
Milligan	10	0-2	0-0	1	4	1	0
M.Johnson	20	1-3	0-0	2	1	0	3
Conklin	8	1-4	0-0	3	0	1	3
Totals	200	25-68	11-18	43	13	23	66

Three-point goals: 5-16, 31.3 (Marciniak 2-8, Davis 1-1, M. Johnson 1-2, Conklin 1-4, McCray 0-1). **FG pct.:** 36.3; **FT pct.:** 61.1. **Team rebounds:** 6. **TO:** 25. **Blocks:** 0. **Steals:** 9 (T. Johnson 3). **Fouled out:** Davis.

Connecticut

Player	M	FG	FT	RB	A	PF	T
Elliott	37	4-11	4-5	6	4	2	12
Lobo	27	5-11	2-2	6	4	5	13
Wolters	34	7-14	4-5	4	1	2	18
Rizzotti	39	6-12	3-4	4	4	3	17
Webber	10	0-0	0-1	4	3	0	0
Sales	29	5-10	0-1	3	3	0	12
Berube	21	2-4	1-4	3	1	3	5
Better	3	0-0	0-0	2	0	0	0
Totals	200	29-62	14-22	43	20	15	77

Three-point goals: 5-16, 31.3 (Sales 2-4, Rizzotti 2-5, Lobo 1-4, Elliott 0-3). **FG pct.:** 46.8; **FT pct.:** 63.6. **Team rebounds:** 9. **TO:** 20. **Blocks:** 10 (Lobo 5, Wolters 5). **Steals:** 11 (Rizzotti 5). **Fouled out:** Lobo.

Halftime — UConn, 41-33.
Officials — Yvette McKinney, Frank Geiselman, Angie Sanseviro.
Attendance — 8,241 at Gampel Pavilion, Storrs

Game 14
Jan. 18
UConn 79
Boston College 54

Connecticut

Player	M	FG	FT	RB	A	PF	T
Elliott	24	0-5	3-4	3	1	1	3
Lobo	22	3-7	1-3	3	1	4	7
Wolters	20	5-7	4-5	6	1	1	14
Rizzotti	23	6-12	2-2	1	2	2	16
Webber	26	2-3	0-2	2	4	2	5
Sales	23	4-9	0-2	10	1	3	9
Berube	17	5-7	3-4	3	2	1	13
Better	17	1-3	2-5	4	1	1	4
Rose	13	0-1	0-1	2	0	0	0
Marquis	7	2-3	0-0	1	0	3	4
Hunt	5	2-2	0-1	1	0	0	4
Gelfenbien	3	0-0	0-0	1	0	0	0
Totals	200	30-59	15-29	41	13	18	79

Three-point goals: 4-13, 30.8 (Rizzotti 2-5, Sales 1-2, Webber 1-3, Berube 0-1, Elliott 0-2). FG pct.: 50.8; FT pct.: 51.7. Team rebounds: 4. TO: 17. Blocks: 2 (Wolters, Sales). Steals: 12 (Sales 4). Technical foul: bench.

Boston College

Player	M	FG	FT	RB	A	PF	T
Porter	33	3-12	6-9	10	0	4	12
Cohen	34	1-4	0-2	4	1	5	3
Campbell	24	4-10	1-2	2	2	4	9
Beezer	29	4-10	0-1	6	3	2	8
Squair	14	1-1	0-2	2	1	2	2
O'Connor	24	6-11	1-3	5	0	3	14
McCormck	32	1-3	0-0	6	1	3	2
Gallagher	4	0-0	0-0	1	0	1	0
Bowersox	2	1-1	0-0	0	0	0	2
Passanno	2	0-2	0-0	0	0	1	0
Crowder	2	1-3	0-1	1	0	0	2
Totals	200	22-57	8-20	40	8	25	54

Three-point goals: 2-6, 33.3 (O'Connor 1-1, Cohen 1-1, Beezer 0-1, Passanno 0-1, Porter 0-2). FG pct.: 38.6; FT pct.: 40.0. Team rebounds: 3. TO: 28. Blocks: 6 (Cohen 3). Steals: 10 (Porter 5). Fouled out: Cohen.

Halftime — UConn, 51-24
Officials — Janice Aliberti, John Jones
Attendance — 2,415 at Conte Forum, Chestnut Hill, Mass.

Game 15
Jan. 22
UConn 89
Syracuse 58

Syracuse

Player	M	FG	FT	RB	A	PF	T
Mumby	25	0-4	4-4	6	0	3	4
McCory	32	8-17	0-0	10	0	4	17
Masimini	22	3-13	2-4	6	2	5	8
Cook	40	7-16	2-4	7	4	1	17
Nurse	27	2-7	0-0	4	1	2	5
Schildt	10	0-1	0-2	2	0	2	0
Glover	16	1-5	1-2	4	0	2	3
Duffy	11	1-2	0-0	2	1	0	2
Angelina	9	0-2	0-0	1	1	2	0
Gooden	4	1-2	0-0	0	1	0	2
Hicks	4	0-1	0-0	0	0	1	0
Totals	200	23-70	9-16	46	10	22	58

Three-point goals: 3-8 (Cook 1-1, McCory 1-2, Nurse 1-2, Duffy 0-1, Angelina 0-1, Gooden 0-1). FG pct.: 32.9; FT pct.: 56.3. Team rebounds: 4. TO: 22. Steals: 2 (McCory, Nurse). Blocks: 1 (Schildt). Fouled out: Masimini. Technical foul: bench

Connecticut

Player	M	FG	FT	RB	A	PF	T
Berube	23	3-7	3-4	6	0	3	9
Elliott	21	4-9	1-2	6	1	4	9
Lobo	28	7-17	0-0	14	4	2	14
Rizzotti	23	3-7	12-12	4	6	2	19
Webber	29	1-3	0-0	0	5	0	3
Better	17	1-3	1-2	4	2	0	3
Sales	16	4-6	0-0	5	1	3	9
Wolters	21	4-10	6-7	5	4	1	14
Rose	9	1-3	2-2	0	0	1	5
Marquis	5	1-2	0-0	0	0	1	2
Hunt	4	0-1	2-4	1	0	0	2
Gelfenbien	4	0-0	0-0	0	0	0	0
Totals	200	29-68	27-33	50	23	17	89

Three-point goals: 4-9 (Sales 1-1, Rose 1-2, Webber 1-2, Rizzotti 1-3, Lobo 0-1). FG pct.: 42.7; FT pct.: 81.8. Team rebounds: 5. TO: 15. Steals: 17 (Rizzotti 6). Blocks: 9 (Lobo 6).

Halftime — UConn, 43-27
Officials — Pat Sullivan, Larry Savo
Attendance — 8,241 at Gampel Pavilion, Storrs

Game 16
Jan. 24
UConn 92
Miami 51

Connecticut

Player	M	FG	FT	RB	A	PF	T
Elliott	30	4-7	2-4	13	2	1	10
Lobo	32	6-21	5-7	6	5	1	17
Wolters	30	7-12	0-0	8	0	2	14
Rizzotti	27	3-7	0-0	7	6	0	7
Webber	25	6-9	0-0	2	2	0	14
Sales	10	3-5	1-3	4	2	3	7
Berube	14	5-10	1-2	5	1	2	11
Better	15	1-6	3-5	2	0	2	5
Rose	6	0-2	1-2	1	1	1	1
Gelfenbien	3	0-0	0-0	0	0	0	0
Hunt	4	1-1	1-2	2	0	0	3
Marquis	4	1-1	1-1	0	0	0	3
Totals	200	37-81	15-26	57	19	12	92

Three-point goals: 3-13 (Webber 2-5, Rizzotti 1-3, Lobo 0-1, Better 0-3, Berube 0-1). FG pct.: .457; FT pct.: .577. Team rebounds: 7. TO: 17 (Elliott 4). Blocks: 10 (Wolters 5, Lobo 4). Steals: 11 (Elliott 2, Lobo 2, Rizzotti 2, Better 2).

Miami

Player	M	FG	FT	RB	A	PF	T
Blue	34	5-16	3-6	10	0	5	13
Young	17	2-6	0-0	5	2	1	4
Jordan	27	3-12	3-4	3	1	1	9
Zaltz	14	1-7	0-0	3	0	2	2
Faulkner	11	0-2	0-0	0	1	1	0
Olson	6	1-2	0-0	0	0	0	2
S. Murray	29	5-12	0-0	6	1	2	10
M. Murray	15	1-4	2-2	3	0	1	5
Henne	7	0-1	0-0	0	0	0	0
Wimes	29	3-7	0-0	7	3	5	6
Schmid	11	0-2	0-0	1	0	1	0
Totals	200	21-71	8-12	43	8	19	51

Three-point goals: 1-7 (M. Murray 1-4, Zaltz 0-1, Faulkner 0-1, Schmid 0-1). FG pct.: .296; FT pct.: .667. Team rebounds: 5. TO: 23. Steals: 6 (Zaltz 2, Wimes 2). Blocks: 5 (Blue 2, Jordan 2). Fouled out: Blue, Wimes.

Halftime — UConn, 48-27
Officials — Yvette McKinney, Kathy Lynch.
Attendance — 921 at Knight Sports Complex, Coral Gables, Fla.

Game 17
Jan. 28
UConn 97
Kansas 87

Connecticut

Player	M	FG	FT	RB	A	PF	T
Elliott	29	4-8	2-2	12	2	5	10
Lobo	36	9-17	7-9	12	6	2	25
Wolters	23	3-11	2-3	8	1	2	8
Rizzotti	34	7-14	5-7	2	7	4	21
Webber	20	2-3	0-0	2	1	2	6
Sales	29	7-12	2-2	8	2	2	21
Berube	27	2-12	2-2	6	3	0	6
Better	2	0-0	0-0	0	0	0	0
Totals	200	34-77	20-25	52	22	17	97

Three-point goals: 9-22, 40.9 (Sales 5-7, Webber 2-3, Rizzotti 2-7, Elliott 0-1, Lobo 0-2, Berube 0-2). **FG pct.:** 44.2; **FT pct.:** 80.0. **Team rebounds:** 2. **TO:** 12. **Blocks:** 5 (Wolters 3). **Steals:** 6 (Rizzotti 3). **Fouled out:** Elliott.

Kansas

Player	M	FG	FT	RB	A	PF	T
Sampson	35	6-10	3-4	8	2	4	19
Aycock	38	9-22	5-6	14	1	5	29
Trapp	35	0-5	0-0	2	3	4	0
Halbleib	33	2-12	2-3	8	1	2	7
Dixon	35	12-22	5-8	6	6	1	30
Canada	10	0-1	0-0	1	0	1	0
Gracey	10	1-2	0-0	1	1	1	2
Moffite	4	0-1	0-0	0	0	0	0
Totals	200	30-75	15-21	43	14	18	87

Three-point goals: 12-28, 42.9 (Aycock 6-9, Sampson 4-8, Dixon 1-4, Halbleib 1-7). **FG pct.:** 40.0; **FT pct.:** 71.4. **Team rebounds:** 3. **TO:** 15. **Blocks:** 3 (Dixon 2). **Steals:** 6 (Aycock 3). **Fouled out:** Aycock.

Halftime — UConn, 47-35.
Officials — Albert Titus, Dennis DeMayo, Yvette McKinney.
Attendance — 16,981 at Kemper Arena, Kansas City, Mo.

Game 18
Jan. 31
UConn 89
Providence 56

Connecticut

Player	M	FG	FT	RB	A	PF	T
Berube	29	7-14	2-5	9	3	3	17
Elliott	24	4-6	1-2	13	4	4	10
Lobo	32	7-20	2-4	9	4	1	16
Rizzotti	32	8-11	0-2	0	2	1	19
Webber	24	3-6	0-1	3	3	2	8
Better	10	3-5	1-3	4	1	0	7
Rose	8	0-3	0-0	1	1	0	0
Marquis	8	1-1	0-0	1	0	3	2
Hunt	4	1-1	1-2	5	0	0	3
Gelfenbien	3	1-1	0-0	1	0	1	2
Sales	26	2-8	0-0	5	2	0	5
Totals	200	37-76	7-19	57	20	15	89

Three-point goals: 8-16, 50.0 (Rizzotti 3-6, Webber 2-3, Berube 1-2, Elliott 1-1, Lobo 0-1, Sales 1-3). **FG pct.:** 48.7 ; **FT pct.:** 36.8. **Team rebounds:** 6. **TO:** 13 (Lobo 3, Berube 2, Elliott 2, Rizzotti, Webber, Marquis, Hunt, Sales 2). **Blocks:** 6 (Lobo 3, Sales 2, Gelfenbien). **Steals:** 13 (Rizzotti 6, Berube 2, Lobo 2, Sales 2, Better).

Providence

Player	M	FG	FT	RB	A	PF	T
Miller	31	5-10	1-4	8	3	3	11
Chatten	24	3-11	4-4	10	3	3	11
Penrod	28	7-8	1-3	7	2	4	15
Bresnahan	23	0-6	0-0	2	0	3	0
Wheeler	33	3-13	0-0	5	2	0	9
Cavallo	25	0-7	0-0	0	2	2	0
Malone	2	0-0	0-0	0	0	0	0
Moyano	34	4-12	0-0	4	1	2	10
Totals	200	22-67	6-11	38	13	17	56

Three-point goals: 6-30, 20.0 (Chatten 1-2, Bresnahan 0-3, Wheeler 3-13, Cavallo 0-5, Moyano 2-7). **FG pct.:** 32.8; **FT pct.:** 54.5. **Team rebounds:** 2. **TO:** 21 (Miller 5, Chatten, Penrod, Bresnahan 4, Wheeler 4, Cavallo 2, Moyano). **Blocks:** 3 (Miller Chatten, Penrod). **Steals:** 4 (Miller, Bresnahan, Wheeler, Moyano).

Halftime — UConn, 38-34.
Officials — Jack Riordan, Tom Danaher.
Attendance — 2,013 at Alumni Hall, Providence

Game 19
Feb. 5
UConn 94
Georgetown 72

Georgetown

Player	M	G	FT	RB	A	PF	T
Pendrghst	31	6-19	2-2	7	0	2	17
Jacobsen	31	6-16	0-0	10	0	4	13
LaForce	16	1-10	1-2	4	0	3	3
Williams	31	2-6	2-3	9	5	4	6
Hanrahan	33	1-8	3-3	3	2	0	6
Gallon	24	6-12	2-2	0	1	1	17
Akonkhai	24	3-7	4-4	5	0	4	10
Staier	9	0-0	0-0	1	0	1	0
Nixon	1	0-0	0-0	0	0	0	0
Totals	200	25-78	14-16	43	8	19	72

Three-point goals: 8-23 (Penderghast 3-6, Gallon 3-7, Jacobsen 1-5, Hanrahan 1-5). **FG pct.:** 32.1; **FT pct.:** 87.5. **Team rebounds:** 4. **TO:** 26. **Steals:** 9 (Jacobsen 3). **Blocks:** 2 (LaForce, Akonkhai).

Connecticut

Player	M	FG	FT	RB	A	PF	T
Elliott	30	6-10	6-7	13	6	1	19
Sales	25	3-11	1-3	4	4	3	8
Lobo	28	15-21	2-7	14	5	1	33
Rizzotti	26	3-7	0-1	2	7	2	7
Webber	31	2-3	2-3	3	5	0	7
Berube	23	4-8	1-2	5	1	4	10
Better	16	3-7	0-1	2	0	1	6
Rose	8	1-5	0-0	0	1	1	2
Hunt	6	1-3	0-0	3	1	0	2
Marquis	4	0-0	0-0	0	0	0	0
Gelfenbien	3	0-0	0-0	3	0	0	0
Totals	200	38-75	12-24	55	30	13	94

Three-point goals: 6-15 (Elliott 1-2, Lobo 1-2, Webber 1-2, Berube 1-2, Sales 1-3, Rizzotti 1-4). **FG pct.:** 50.7; **FT pct.:** 50.0. **Team rebounds:** 6. **TO:** 24. **Steals:** 13 (Sales 5). **Blocks:** 6 (Lobo 6).

Halftime — UConn, 45-28
Officials — Frank Geiselman, Deborah Allen.
Attendance — 8,241 at Gampel Pavilion, Storrs

Game 20
Feb. 9
UConn 85
Miami 48

Miami

Player	M	FG	FT	RB	A	PF	T
Blue	24	2-10	2-2	3	0	4	6
S. Murray	35	5-18	0-0	5	0	4	10
Olson	8	0-2	0-0	0	1	2	0
Zaltz	37	7-17	4-4	5	2	3	18
Faulkner	19	0-2	0-0	1	1	5	0
Young	21	3-7	1-2	2	1	5	7
Jordan	10	0-1	0-0	0	0	2	0
Wimes	27	3-6	0-1	5	1	3	6
Henne	2	0-0	0-0	0	0	0	0
Schmid	12	0-1	1-2	1	0	0	1
M. Murray	2	0-0	0-0	1	0	1	0
Toomer	1	0-0	0-0	0	0	0	0
Wagner	2	0-0	0-0	0	0	0	0
Totals	200	20-64	8-11	32	6	29	48

Three-point goals: 0-4, 00.0 (Zaltz 0-4). **FG pct.:** 31.3; **FT pct.:** 72.7. **Team rebounds:** 9. **TO:** 20 (S. Murray 4, Zaltz 4, Blue 3, Faulkner 3, Young 3, Wimes 3). **Blocks:** 2 (Blue, Zaltz). **Steals:** 6 (Young 2, S. Murray, Zaltz, Jordan, Wimes). **Fouled out:** Faulkner.

Connecticut

Player	M	FG	FT	RB	A	PF	T
Elliott	33	2-5	6-6	6	5	1	10
Sales	27	4-10	3-6	4	3	1	13
Lobo	29	8-15	3-3	11	3	1	19
Rizzotti	27	4-7	0-0	2	6	2	10
Webber	17	1-2	3-4	2	2	3	6
Berube	18	5-9	3-6	2	1	2	13
Wolters	16	3-4	4-7	8	2	2	10
Better	16	0-3	1-4	3	0	1	1
Rose	7	1-1	0-0	0	0	1	3
Gelfenbien	4	0-1	0-0	2	0	0	0
Marquis	3	0-0	0-0	0	0	1	0
Hunt	3	0-0	0-0	0	0	0	0
Totals	200	28-57	23-36	51	22	15	85

Three-point goals: 6-13, 46.2 (Sales 2-4, Rizzotti 2-5, Webber 1-2, Rose 1-1, Lobo 0-1). **FG pct.:** 49.1; **FT pct.:** 63.9. **Team rebounds:** 11. **TO:** 19 (Lobo 4, Webber 3, Better 3, Elliott 2, Sales 2, Berube 2, Rizzotti, Rose, Gelfenbien). **Blocks:** 10 (Lobo 8, Wolters 2). **Steals:** 9 (Sales 3, Berube 3, Rizzotti 2, Lobo).

Halftime — UConn, 43-14
Officials — Phyllis Deveney, Alonza Gray
Attendance — 8,241 at Gampel Pavilion, Storrs

Game 21
Feb. 12
UConn 84
Seton Hall 62

Connecticut

Player	M	FG	FT	RB	A	PF	T
Elliott	25	3-9	2-2	8	3	5	8
Lobo	37	7-15	4-7	11	5	2	18
Wolters	22	5-9	0-1	5	2	5	10
Webber	18	0-2	0-0	0	4	3	0
Rizzotti	37	6-16	3-4	4	6	3	18
Sales	28	7-12	0-0	4	3	2	15
Berube	26	4-7	5-6	6	2	2	14
Better	6	0-0	1-2	2	0	0	1
Rose	1	0-0	0-0	0	0	0	0
Totals	200	32-70	15-22	44	25	22	84

Three-point goals: 5-19 (Rizzotti 3-10, Sales 1-3, Berube 1-3, Lobo 0-1). **FG pct.:** 45.7; **FT pct.:** 68.2. **Team rebounds:** 4. **TO:** 16. **Steals:** 15 (Sales 4, Elliott 4). **Blocks:** 5 (Lobo 4). **Fouled out:** Elliott, Wolters.

Seton Hall

Player	M	FG	FT	RB	A	PF	T
Quinney	33	2-6	0-1	5	4	3	4
Wynne	37	3-8	7-10	15	2	4	13
Johnson	35	6-12	6-6	4	3	4	18
Mitchell	31	4-13	4-6	4	4	4	15
Heins	35	3-11	0-0	6	3	2	6
Walker	14	1-5	0-0	1	0	1	2
Turner	2	0-1	0-0	0	0	0	0
Makarewicz	13	2-4	0-0	3	0	1	4
Totals	200	21-60	17-23	41	16	19	62

Three-point goals: 3-9 (Mitchell 3-6, Heins 0-3). **FG pct.:** 35.0; **FT pct.:** 73.9. **Team rebounds:** 3. **TO:** 23. **Steals:** 9 (Wynne 5). **Blocks:** 4 (Wynne 2, Johnson 2).

Halftime — UConn, 45-29.
Officials — Janice Aliberti, Dennis DeMayo.
Attendance — 3,200 at Walsh Gym, South Orange, N.J.

Game 22
Feb. 16
UConn 71
Pittsburgh 43

Connecticut

Player	M	FG	FT	RB	A	PF	T
Elliott	27	1-6	3-5	4	2	1	5
Lobo	26	11-15	3-3	4	6	1	26
Wolters	22	6-11	1-2	4	0	3	13
Rizzotti	27	0-8	2-2	3	4	1	2
Webber	27	1-4	1-2	3	6	2	3
Better	14	0-0	3-4	5	1	1	3
Rose	13	0-2	0-0	2	0	1	0
Marquis	3	1-1	1-2	0	0	1	3
Berube	11	2-4	4-4	3	0	0	8
Hunt	7	0-2	0-2	4	0	1	0
Gelfenbien	3	0-0	0-0	1	0	0	0
Sales	20	3-7	2-2	6	1	1	8
Totals	200	25-60	20-28	44	20	13	71

Three-point goals: 1-13, 7.7 (Lobo 1-1, Rizzotti 0-5, Webber 0-3, Sales 0-2, Elliott 0-1, Rose 0-1). **FG pct.:** 41.7; **FT pct.:** 71.4. **Team rebounds:** 5. **TO:** 13 (Berube 3, Wolters 2, Better 2, Hunt 2, Lobo, Rizzotti, Webber, Sales). **Blocks:** 3 (Lobo, Hunt, Sales). **Steals:** 10 (Rizzotti 2, Berube 2, Sales 2, Elliott, Lobo, Better, Rose).

Pittsburgh

Player	M	FG	FT	RB	A	PF	T
Joyce	23	1-7	2-2	2	1	3	4
Bolfert	26	2-4	0-0	6	0	0	4
Howard	23	2-6	0-1	4	0	4	4
Petho	26	1-7	1-2	6	2	0	4
Morton	28	3-11	0-0	5	1	4	6
Guzman	5	2-6	0-0	1	1	1	4
Warren	5	1-3	0-0	0	1	0	2
Fornadel	19	1-5	2-2	5	1	4	4
Miller	20	2-8	0-0	2	0	2	6
Senneca	12	1-1	0-0	1	0	0	2
Woods	13	0-1	3-4	4	0	3	3
Totals	200	16-59	8-11	42	7	21	43

Three-point goals: 3-14, 21.4 (Miller 2-7, Petho 1-1, Guzman 0-3, Joyce 0-2, Morton 0-1). **FG pct.:** 27.1; **FT pct.:** 72.7. **Team rebounds:** 6. **TO:** 24 (Morton 11, Petho 3, Joyce 2, Miller 2, Howard 2, Bolfert, Fornadel, Senneca). **Blocks:** 2 (Fornadel, Woods). **Steals:** 6 (Morton 3, Bolfert. Petho, Fornadel).

Halftime — UConn, 41-22
Officials — John Jones, Peter Rodriquez
Attendance — 1,896 at Fitzgerald Field House, Pittsburgh

Game 23
Feb. 19
UConn 86
Boston College 34

Boston College

Player	M	FG	FT	RB	A	PF	T
Porter	31	6-15	0-0	4	3	5	13
Cohen	40	2-16	0-0	7	1	2	4
O'Connor	14	1-5	1-2	1	0	5	3
Gallagher	28	1-6	0-0	2	0	1	2
McCrmick	37	0-4	0-0	8	3	3	0
Campbell	16	2-7	0-0	1	0	0	4
Beezer	24	1-6	1-2	1	1	1	3
Bowersox	1	0-0	0-0	1	0	0	0
Crowder	4	2-2	1-2	0	0	1	5
Passanno	3	0-1	0-0	0	0	1	0
Squair	2	0-0	0-0	0	0	0	0
Totals	200	15-62	3-6	30	8	19	34

Three-point goals: 1-9 (Porter 1-2, Passanno 0-1, Beezer 0-2, Gallagher 0-4). **FG pct.:** 24.2; **FT pct.:** 50.0. **Team rebounds:** 5. **TO:** 24. **Steals:** 4 (Cohen, O'Connor, McCormick, Beezer) **Blocks:** 3 (Campbell 2). **Fouled out:** Porter, O'Connor.

Connecticut

Player	M	FG	FT	RB	A	PF	T
Elliott	25	2-7	4-4	9	4	1	8
Lobo	23	9-17	0-0	12	0	3	18
Wolters	25	3-10	0-0	10	1	2	6
Rizzotti	21	3-6	0-1	0	4	0	9
Webber	28	2-3	2-2	3	7	1	8
Sales	19	4-5	0-0	3	3	1	10
Berube	18	5-7	2-2	5	2	0	12
Better	13	1-4	4-4	2	1	3	7
Rose	13	1-3	0-0	0	0	0	3
Hunt	8	0-2	3-4	3	0	1	3
Marquis	4	0-1	2-2	1	0	0	2
Gelfenbien	3	0-0	0-0	0	0	1	0
Totals	200	30-65	17-19	53	22	13	86

Three-point goals: 9-15 (Rizzotti 3-3, Webber 2-3, Sales 2-3, Rose 1-2, Better 1-3, Lobo 0-1). **FG pct.:** 46.2; **FT pct.:** 89.5. **Team rebounds:** 5. **TO:** 20. **Steals:** 13 (Sales 6). **Blocks:** 10 (Wolters 8)

Halftime — UConn, 44-19
Officials — Bob McEntee, Al Gray
Attendance — 8,241 at Gampel Pavilion, Storrs

Game 24
Feb. 22
UConn 103
St. John's 56

St. John's

Player	M	FG	FT	RB	A	PF	T
Kelly	19	0-8	1-2	3	1	2	1
Oliver	25	0-5	0-0	3	0	1	0
Lattanzio	30	2-6	1-3	5	0	2	5
Price	32	4-9	0-0	2	3	1	9
Jackson	31	7-15	3-4	4	1	3	18
Miller	17	1-5	2-2	4	2	2	4
Schell	21	3-14	4-4	5	0	2	11
Burke	16	3-8	0-0	2	1	4	6
Crockett	9	1-5	0-0	2	0	3	2
Totals	200	21-75	11-15	33	8	20	56

Three-point goals: 3-21, 14.3 (Jackson 1-2, Price 1-5, Schell 1-9, Burke 0-1, Kelly 0-2, Miller 0-2). **FG pct.:** 28.0; **FT pct.:** 73.3. **Team rebounds:** 3. **TO:** 14. **Blocks:** 3 (Kelly, Price, Crockett). **Steals:** 7 (Price 2).

Connecticut

Player	M	FG	FT	RB	A	PF	T
Elliott	20	1-4	0-1	9	4	1	2
Gelfenbien	9	0-2	2-2	2	0	1	2
Lobo	28	6-14	1-4	16	4	2	13
Rizzotti	26	5-9	1-1	1	3	2	14
Webber	26	2-3	4-4	3	4	3	9
Wolters	21	9-13	2-2	6	3	1	20
Sales	17	6-10	0-1	4	2	0	13
Berube	16	4-7	4-5	6	4	3	12
Better	15	1-2	0-0	3	2	1	2
Rose	11	2-2	2-2	2	1	0	6
Hunt	8	2-4	0-0	1	0	0	4
Marquis	3	3-3	0-0	1	0	0	6
Totals	200	41-73	16-22	60	27	14	103

Three-point goals: 5-11, 45.5 (Rizzotti 3-5, Webber 1-2, Sales 1-2, Lobo 0-2). **FG pct.:** 56.2; **FT pct.:** 72.7. **Team rebounds:** 6. **TO:** 16. **Blocks:** 9 (Lobo 7). **Steals:** 8 (Sales 4).

Halftime — UConn, 47-24
Officials — Angie Sanseviro, Kathy Lynch.
Attendance — 8,241 at Gampel Pavilion, Storrs

Game 25
Feb. 25
UConn 89
Syracuse 62

Connecticut

Player	M	FG	FT	RB	A	PF	T
Elliott	27	4-7	3-4	7	1	2	11
Lobo	31	9-16	6-6	6	2	0	25
Wolters	21	8-13	0-1	4	1	3	16
Rizzotti	27	3-9	2-2	2	8	1	10
Webber	23	1-6	2-2	1	4	0	4
Better	13	1-1	1-2	4	1	1	3
Rose	12	0-2	0-0	0	3	1	0
Marquis	3	1-2	0-1	1	0	2	2
Berube	11	2-3	4-4	3	2	4	9
Hunt	8	0-1	0-2	2	2	2	0
Gelfenbien	3	0-1	0-0	0	0	0	0
Sales	21	3-4	2-3	6	0	3	9
Totals	200	32-65	20-27	41	24	19	89

Three-point goals: 5-12 (Rizzotti 2-6, Lobo 1-1, Berube 1-1 Sales 1-1, Webber 0-3). **FG pct.:** 49.2; **FT pct.:** 74.1. **Team rebounds:** 5. **TO:** 19. **Steals:** 10 (Rizzotti 7). **Blocks:** 2 (Lobo, Wolters).

Syracuse

Player	M	FG	FT	RB	A	PF	T
Glover	26	3-6	3-4	4	0	3	9
Duffy	40	7-18	3-3	5	1	3	18
Masimini	33	7-15	1-1	5	1	5	15
Mumby	31	2-6	2-4	3	4	3	6
Nurse	37	3-11	1-2	10	4	4	7
Gooden	6	0-1	0-0	1	1	0	0
Hicks	3	1-2	1-1	2	0	0	3
McCory	21	2-8	0-1	2	2	4	4
Angelina	3	0-0	0-0	0	2	0	0
Totals	200	25-67	11-16	42	15	22	62

Three-point goals: 1-8 (Duffy 1-5, Mumby 0-1, Hicks 0-1, Nurse 0-1). **FG pct.:** 37.3; **FT pct.:** 68.8. **Team rebounds:** 10. **TO:** 26. **Steals:** 8 (Nurse, Duffy 2). **Fouled out:** Masimini.

Halftime — UConn, 41-30
Officials — Bill Titus, Kevin Collier
Attendance — 3,517 at Manley Field House, Syracuse, N.Y.

Game 26
Feb. 27
UConn 79
Villanova 54

Connecticut

Player	M	FG	FT	RB	A	PF	T
Elliott	30	4-6	0-0	8	2	2	10
Lobo	29	4-9	2-3	6	3	1	10
Wolters	27	12-17	2-2	3	0	1	26
Rizzotti	29	3-6	2-2	6	6	1	8
Webber	28	1-3	6-6	1	6	0	9
Sales	19	4-5	0-0	2	0	3	9
Berube	12	0-3	0-1	2	0	1	0
Better	7	1-2	2-3	2	0	2	4
Rose	6	1-1	0-2	3	0	0	2
Hunt	6	0-1	1-3	2	0	0	1
Marquis	4	0-1	0-0	0	0	0	0
Gelfenbien	3	0-0	0-0	0	0	1	0
Totals	200	30-54	15-22	38	17	12	79

Three-point goals: 4-10 (Elliott 2-2, Sales 1-2, Webber 1-3 Lobo 0-1, Rizzotti 0-1, Berube 0-1).
FG pct.: 55.6.; **FT pct.:** 68.2. **Team rebounds:** 3.
TO: 17. **Blocks:** 5 (Lobo 3). **Steals:** 8 (Sales 4).

Villanova

Player	M	FG	FT	RB	A	PF	T
Baglio	26	2-7	0-0	3	1	3	5
Snell	21	1-7	0-0	4	1	3	2
Maga	31	4-10	0-0	9	1	2	8
Glenning	31	5-14	2-2	2	4	3	14
Thornton	31	1-8	2-2	1	5	1	4
Rosenthal	14	2-4	0-0	6	0	4	4
Beisel	16	1-3	0-0	2	3	1	2
Higgins	11	3-6	0-0	3	0	0	6
Keffer	12	3-5	0-0	1	0	2	9
Bradshaw	3	0-1	0-0	0	0	0	0
Hightower	4	0-0	0-0	0	1	0	0
Totals	200	22-65	4-4	34	16	19	54

Three-point goals: 6-21 (Keffer 3-3, Glenning 2-8, Baglio 1-3, Higgins 0-2, Thornton 0-5). **FG pct.:** 33.8 ;
FT pct.: 100.0. **Team rebounds:** 3. **TO:** 22.
Blocks: 1 (Maga). **Steals:** 6 (Thornton 3).

Halftime — UConn, 40-21
Officials — Janice Aliberti, Dennis DeMayo
Attendance — 3,622 at duPont Pavilion, Villanova, Pa.

Game 27
March 4
Big East quarterfinal
UConn 92
Providence 63

Providence

Player	M	FG	FT	RB	A	PF	T
Chatten	28	4-11	1-2	5	2	1	9
Miller	21	2-4	2-2	5	2	5	6
Penrod	30	2-2	0-0	2	1	1	4
Wheeler	35	4-8	0-0	2	4	2	11
Moyano	25	3-8	0-0	3	2	4	9
Cavallo	15	2-5	0-0	2	1	0	6
Malone	1	0-0	0-0	0	0	0	0
Bresnahan	13	1-6	0-0	0	1	2	3
Malcolm	32	6-16	3-6	8	2	2	15
Totals	200	24-60	6-10	29	15	17	63

Three-point goals: 9-22 (Wheeler 3-6, Moyano 3-6, Cavallo 2-4, Bresnahan 1-3, Chatten 0-1, Malcolm 0-2). **FG pct.:** 40.0; **FT pct.:** 60.0. **Team rebounds:** 2.
TO: 30. **Steals:** 7 (Cavallo 3). **Blocks:** 1 (Moyano).
Fouled out: Miller.

Connecticut

Player	M	FG	FT	RB	A	PF	T
Elliott	30	3-4	1-2	9	4	3	7
Lobo	30	9-16	2-3	12	3	1	23
Wolters	29	9-12	1-1	2	2	4	19
Rizzotti	19	5-6	4-4	1	2	0	15
Webber	29	3-5	0-0	4	5	0	8
Better	9	0-0	0-0	0	0	1	0
Marquis	2	0-0	0-0	0	0	0	0
Gelfenbien	2	0-0	0-0	0	0	1	0
Rose	7	1-2	0-0	0	1	0	2
Sales	19	5-9	1-1	4	6	3	11
Hunt	4	2-3	0-0	0	0	1	4
Berube	20	1-8	1-2	4	2	0	3
Totals	200	38-65	10-13	38	25	14	92

Three-point goals: 6-13 (Lobo 3-4, Webber 2-4, Rizzotti 1-1, Sales 0-2, Berube 0-2). **FG pct.:** 58.5; **FT pct.:** 76.9. **Team rebounds:** 2. **TO:** 25.
Steals: 18 (Sales 5). **Blocks:** 10 (Wolters 6).

Halftime — UConn, 54-28
Officials — Yvette McKinney, Jack Plunkett, Jack Riordan.
Attendance — 1,950 at Walsh Gym, South Orange, N.J.

Game 28
March 5
Big East semifinal
UConn 95
Pittsburgh 63

Pittsburgh

Player	M	FG	FT	RB	A	PF	T
Bolfert	15	0-1	0-0	1	1	1	0
Joyce	31	1-7	2-2	1	1	2	4
Howard	25	4-14	3-5	6	0	4	11
Morton	31	3-11	0-0	3	8	2	6
Petho	24	6-12	4-5	6	1	1	16
Fornadel	10	1-6	2-2	2	1	4	4
Guzman	5	0-1	0-0	1	0	2	0
Senneca	12	2-2	0-0	2	0	1	4
Warren	6	1-2	1-2	1	0	0	4
Miller	17	1-6	0-0	0	2	3	2
Woods	24	5-10	2-2	9	0	2	12
Totals	200	24-72	14-18	35	14	22	63

Three-point goals: 1-11, 09.1 (Warren 1-1, Petho 0-1, Guzman 0-1, Joyce 0-2, Morton 0-2, Miller 0-4).
FG pct.: 33.3; **FT pct.:** 77.8. **Team rebounds:** 3. **TO:** 20 (Joyce 3, Bolfert 2, Howard 2, Morton 2, Petho 2, Fornadel 2, Guzman 2, Senneca 2, Miller 2). **Blocks:** 3 (Joyce, Howard, Woods). **Steals:** 12 (Howard 4, Morton 3).

Connecticut

Player	M	FG	FT	RB	A	PF	T
Elliott	28	2-5	4-4	4	2	3	8
Lobo	25	7-13	6-7	10	2	1	20
Wolters	23	12-15	1-2	6	0	3	25
Rizzotti	22	4-9	0-1	1	7	2	10
Webber	29	1-2	0-1	3	4	0	3
Sales	21	4-9	1-2	8	6	1	9
Berube	22	4-5	2-3	4	3	3	10
Better	9	2-3	0-0	2	3	1	4
Rose	6	0-2	0-0	0	0	1	0
Gelfenbien	3	0-0	0-0	2	0	0	0
Hunt	5	1-1	2-2	0	0	1	4
Marquis	7	1-1	0-0	0	0	0	2
Totals	200	38-65	16-22	45	27	16	95

Three-point goals: 3-10, 30.0 (Rizzotti 2-4, Webber 1-2, Lobo 0-1, Better 0-1, Sales 0-2). **FG pct.:** 58.5; **FT pct.:** 72.7. **Team rebounds:** 5. **TO:** 22 (Rizzotti 7, Webber 4, Lobo 3, Better 2, Rose 2). **Blocks:** 5 (Wolters 4, Lobo). **Steals:** 11 (Sales 5, Rizzotti 2).

Halftime — UConn, 52-33
Officials — Bill Titus, Frank Geiselman, Deborah Allen
Attendance — 3,200 at Walsh Gym, South Orange, N.J.

Game 29
March 6
Big East championship
UConn 85
Seton Hall 49

Seton Hall

Player	M	FG	FT	RB	A	PF	T
Wynne	38	4-14	2-2	19	1	4	10
Quinney	39	10-20	0-0	5	0	3	20
Johnson	26	2-10	0-0	3	2	3	4
Heins	35	0-11	0-0	3	2	1	0
Mitchell	17	1-6	2-2	1	4	4	4
Walker	13	1-5	0-0	0	1	1	3
Brookins	8	1-3	0-0	1	0	1	2
Makarewicz	13	2-6	0-0	2	0	3	4
Turner	11	1-3	0-0	1	0	2	2
Totals	200	22-78	4-4	41	10	22	49

Three-point goals: 1-6 (Walker 1-1, Mitchell 0-2, Heins 0-2, Makarewicz 0-1). **FG pct.:** 28.2; **FT pct.:** 100.0. **Team rebounds:** 6. **TO:** 22. **Blocks:** 4 (Wynne 3, Johnson 1). **Steals:** 13 (Wynne, Quinney, Heins 3).

Connecticut

Player	M	FG	FT	RB	A	PF	T
Elliott	27	3-6	0-0	12	5	2	6
Lobo	32	6-14	3-4	10	4	2	15
Wolters	21	13-18	6-8	6	1	0	32
Rizzotti	20	2-3	0-0	0	4	1	5
Webber	21	0-2	0-0	3	3	0	0
Better	15	1-1	2-3	1	1	1	4
Rose	9	0-1	0-1	0	0	1	0
Marquis	7	1-1	0-0	1	0	0	2
Berube	19	5-5	1-2	3	5	1	11
Hunt	5	0-0	0-0	1	0	0	0
Gelfenbien	4	0-2	0-0	0	0	0	0
Sales	20	4-8	2-2	5	4	2	10
Totals	200	35-61	14-20	46	27	10	85

Three-point goals: 1-7 (Rizzotti 1-2, Lobo 0-2, Webber 0-1, Sales 0-1, Marquis 0-1). **FG pct.:** 57.4; **FT pct.:** 70.0. **Team rebounds:** 4. **TO:** 21. **Blocks:** 13 (Lobo, Wolters 6). **Steals:** 15 (Sales 6).

Halftime — UConn, 46-21
Officials — Bill Titus, Frank Geiselman, Dennis DeMayo
Attendance — 3,200 at Walsh Gym, South Orange, N.J.

Game 30
March 16
NCAA first round
UConn 105
Maine 75

Maine

Player	M	FG	FT	RB	A	PF	T
Ripton	27	4-11	1-1	4	1	3	13
Guidi	22	5-11	0-0	5	0	3	10
Porrini	33	4-13	3-4	7	1	5	11
Blodgett	33	4-14	1-1	5	3	2	10
Dionne	22	3-7	1-2	1	1	3	10
Grealy	15	1-4	0-0	1	0	0	2
Gallant	15	3-6	1-2	4	1	2	7
Rustad	9	0-1	0-0	0	0	0	0
Carver	12	4-7	0-0	1	3	0	8
Sullivan	10	1-3	0-0	1	3	1	2
Stubbs	2	1-2	0-0	0	0	0	2
Totals	200	30-79	7-10	35	13	19	75

Three-point goals: 8-22, 36.4 (Ripton 4-10, Dionne 3-6, Blodgett 1-4, Carver 0-1, Stubbs 0-1). **FG pct.:** 38.0; **FT pct.:** 70.0. **Team rebounds:** 6. **TO:** 12 (Blodgett 5, Ripton 2, Gallant 2, Guidi, Porrini, Dionne). **Blocks:** 3 (Guidi 2, Porrini). **Steals:** 7 (Blodgett 2, Sullivan 2, Ripton, Porrini, Grealy). **Fouled out:** Porrini.

Connecticut

Player	M	FG	FT	RB	A	PF	T
Elliott	23	3-9	6-6	9	4	3	13
Lobo	23	8-15	0-5	5	3	2	18
Wolters	25	10-14	3-4	12	1	0	23
Rizzotti	28	4-8	1-2	3	6	3	10
Webber	23	2-2	0-0	0	4	2	5
Sales	22	8-12	0-1	4	2	0	18
Berube	22	1-5	4-4	8	3	2	7
Better	10	1-1	1-3	4	0	3	3
Rose	7	0-1	0-0	1	2	0	0
Hunt	8	1-2	2-3	2	1	2	4
Marquis	5	2-3	0-0	1	0	0	4
Gelfenbien	4	0-1	0-0	0	1	0	0
Totals	200	40-73	17-28	56	27	14	105

Three-point goals: 8-13, 61.5 (Lobo 2-3, Sales 2-3, Elliott 1-1, Webber 1-1, Berube 1-2, Rizzotti 1-3). **FG pct.:** 55.4; **FT pct.:** 60.7. **Team rebounds:** 7. **TO:** 16 (Elliott 3, Rizzotti 3, Rose 3, Berube 2, Lobo 2, Wolters, Webber, Better). **Blocks:** 8 (Lobo 4, Wolters 4). **Steals:** 9 (Lobo 2, Sales 2, Hunt 2, Rizzotti, Berube, Better).

Halftime — UConn, 53-25
Officials — Sally Bell, Mark Zentz
Attendance — 8,241 at Gampel Pavilion, Storrs

Game 31
March 18
NCAA second round
UConn 91
Virginia Tech 45

Virginia Tech

Player	M	FG	FT	RB	A	PF	T
Osborne	36	6-15	5-5	2	2	1	19
Donnell	25	2-6	0-0	2	0	3	4
Root	33	5-11	6-7	7	0	1	16
Garland	30	0-2	0-0	1	3	3	0
Leftwich	26	1-10	0-0	3	1	4	2
Lee	12	1-2	2-4	3	0	4	4
Banks	6	0-0	0-0	0	0	0	0
Hollister	17	0-3	0-0	2	2	2	0
Carter	10	0-4	0-0	2	0	2	0
Nolley	4	0-2	0-0	0	0	0	0
Matlin	1	0-0	0-0	0	0	0	0
Totals	200	15-55	13-16	30	8	20	45

Three-point goals: 2-8, 25.0 (Osborne 2-6, Hollister 0-1, Nolley 0-1). **FG pct.:** 27.3; **FT pct.:** 81.3. **Team rebounds:** 8. **TO:** 29 (Garland 6, Osborne 5, Root 5, Donnell 3, Leftwich 3, Lee 3, Banks 2, Hollister, Carter). **Blocks:** 2 (Osborne, Root). **Steals:** 6 (Donnell 2, Garland, Leftwich, Lee, Carter).

Connecticut

Player	M	FG	FT	RB	A	PF	T
Elliott	26	6-8	3-4	3	3	3	15
Lobo	27	8-13	1-2	11	8	2	17
Wolters	24	8-10	1-1	3	2	3	17
Rizzotti	19	6-7	5-7	2	1	3	20
Webber	26	1-2	0-0	4	7	1	2
Sales	18	3-5	2-2	4	0	2	8
Berube	20	2-7	0-0	6	1	1	4
Better	16	1-4	2-2	0	0	1	4
Hunt	9	1-2	0-1	0	2	1	2
Rose	8	0-0	0-0	0	1	1	0
Marquis	4	1-1	0-0	0	0	1	2
Gelfenbien	3	0-2	0-0	1	0	0	0
Totals	200	37-61	14-19	40	25	19	91

Three-point goals: 3-8, 37.5 (Rizzotti 3-4, Lobo 0-1, Webber 0-1 Sales 0-2). **FG pct.:** 60.7; **FT pct.:** 73.7. **Team rebounds:** 6. **TO:** 20 (Elliott 3, Rizzotti 3, Better 3, Webber 2, Sales 2, Rose 2, Wolters, Lobo, Berube, Hunt). **Blocks:** 9 (Lobo 5, Wolters 3, Elliott). **Steals:** 13 (Sales 5, Elliott 3, Rizzotti 2, Hunt 2).

Halftime — UConn, 45-17
Officials — Judy Stroud, Larry Gasser
Attendance — 8,241 at Gampel Pavilion, Storrs

Game 32
March 23
East Regional semifinal
UConn 87
Alabama 56

Alabama

Player	M	FG	FT	RB	A	PF	T
Johnson	40	4-19	4-4	4	5	1	14
Stevenson	19	1-4	2-2	7	0	3	5
Watkins	29	4-14	3-4	8	2	5	12
Thompson	22	2-8	0-0	0	1	3	5
Ezell	22	1-4	3-3	1	3	2	6
Daniels	16	1-6	0-0	0	0	2	2
Koonce	22	3-8	0-0	5	0	4	6
Smith	14	3-6	0-0	2	0	1	6
Monteith	10	0-1	0-0	2	0	0	0
Duncan	6	0-2	0-0	3	0	0	0
Totals	200	19-72	12-13	36	11	21	56

Three-point goals: 6-27 (Johnson 2-9, Stevenson 1-1, Watkins 1-4, Thompson 1-7, Ezell 1-4, Monteith 0-1, Duncan 0-1). **FG pct.:** 26.4; **FT pct.:** 92.3. **Team rebounds:** 4. **TO:** 14. **Steals:** 8 (Watkins 4). **Blocks:** 4 (Johnson, Watkins, Daniels, Smith). **Fouled out:** Watkins.

Connecticut

Player	M	FG	FT	RB	A	PF	T
Elliott	30	4-7	7-7	14	2	0	15
Lobo	32	6-15	6-8	6	1	3	19
Wolters	25	3-5	3-3	5	0	1	9
Rizzotti	32	10-12	1-1	8	7	4	24
Webber	18	0-3	2-3	3	1	1	2
Sales	19	3-6	0-4	1	0	3	8
Berube	22	1-4	4-4	4	4	1	6
Better	7	1-2	0-0	2	0	1	2
Hunt	6	1-3	0-0	2	0	0	2
Marquis	4	0-3	0-0	2	0	0	0
Rose	3	0-2	0-0	2	1	0	0
Gelfenbien	2	0-0	0-0	0	0	0	0
Totals	200	29-62	23-30	54	16	14	87

Three-point goals: 6-14 (Rizzotti 3-4, Sales 2-4, Lobo 1-2, Webber 0-2, Berube 0-1, Rose 0-1). **FG pct.:** 46.8; **FT pct.:** 76.7. **Team rebounds:** 5. **TO:** 16. **Steals:** 5 (Rizzotti 2). **Blocks:** 4 (Lobo 3).

Halftime — UConn, 51-25
Officials — Larry Sheppard, Kim Balque
Attendance — 8,241 at Gampel Pavilion, Storrs

Game 33
March 25
East Regional championship
UConn 67
Virginia 63

Virginia

Player	M	FG	FT	RB	A	PF	T
Foote	27	2-9	2-2	3	0	4	7
Palmer	35	7-20	4-4	12	1	3	20
Gausepohl	14	2-10	1-2	6	0	1	5
Boucek	29	0-4	3-4	1	1	2	3
Suber	40	3-9	0-0	4	3	1	6
Lofstedt	32	5-6	2-2	3	2	2	14
Beale	23	2-5	4-4	4	1	1	8
Totals	200	21-63	16-18	43	8	14	63

Three-point goals: 5-16, 31.3 (Lofstedt 2-2, Palmer 2-5, Foote 1-5, Suber 0-4). **FG pct.:** 33.3; **FT pct.:** 88.9. **Team rebounds:** 10. **TO:** 16. **Blocks:** 2 (Foote, Beale). **Steals:** 7 (Palmer 3).

Connecticut

Player	M	FG	FT	RB	A	PF	T
Elliott	26	3-5	5-6	8	1	4	12
Lobo	36	3-12	2-2	6	2	3	8
Wolters	32	9-14	0-0	5	0	4	18
Rizzotti	38	6-16	0-0	8	4	4	13
Webber	11	0-2	0-0	0	2	0	0
Sales	31	5-11	0-0	4	3	1	10
Berube	26	2-9	1-3	3	2	1	6
Totals	200	28-69	8-11	41	14	17	67

Three-point goals: 3-17, 17.6 (Elliott 1-1, Berube 1-3, Rizzotti 1-6, Lobo 0-1, Webber 0-2, Sales 0-4). **FG pct.:** 40.6; **FT pct.:** 72.7. **Team rebounds:** 7. **TO:** 15. **Blocks:** 11 (Lobo 6, Wolters 5). **Steals:** 10 (Sales 4).

Halftime — Virginia, 44-37
Officials — Art Bomengen, Marla Denham.
Attendance — 8,241 at Gampel Pavilion, Storrs

Game 34
April 1
NCAA semifinal
UConn 87
Stanford 60

Stanford

Player	M	FG	FT	RB	A	PF	T
Hemmer	20	2-6	1-2	4	0	3	5
Starbird	26	1-9	0-0	3	4	4	2
Kaplan	21	6-11	0-0	7	2	4	12
Paye	37	4-15	0-1	1	9	5	10
Wideman	12	0-3	0-0	4	1	1	0
Mulitauaopl	10	2-7	2-2	4	0	2	6
Folkl	34	5-11	0-0	9	1	3	12
Scott	9	2-6	0-0	1	2	2	4
Owen	5	0-3	0-0	1	0	1	0
Kelsey	4	0-0	0-0	0	1	0	0
Nygaard	11	2-6	0-0	3	0	4	6
Smith	7	1-2	0-0	2	2	1	3
Harrington	2	0-2	0-0	0	0	1	0
Freuen	2	0-2	0-0	1	0	0	0
Totals	200	25-81	3-5	43	22	31	60

Three-point goals: 7-27, 25.9 (Folkl 2-3, Nygaard 2-6, Paye 2-10, Smith 1-2, Harrington 0-1, Starbird 0-3, Wideman 0-1, Freuen 0-1). **FG pct.:** 30.9; **FT pct.:** 60.0. **Team rebounds:** 3. **TO:** 17. **Blocks:** 4 (Folkl 2). **Steals:** 9 (Starbird 3). **Fouled out:** Paye.

Connecticut

Player	M	FG	FT	RB	A	PF	T
Elliott	32	6-9	9-10	6	2	2	21
Lobo	37	5-9	5-6	9	3	1	17
Wolters	33	11-17	9-13	9	2	2	31
Rizzotti	34	1-9	4-8	6	6	0	7
Webber	17	0-1	0-1	1	2	0	0
Sales	15	1-2	3-3	2	2	5	5
Berube	23	0-2	2-2	6	4	2	2
Better	2	0-0	2-2	1	0	1	2
Rose	2	1-1	0-0	0	0	0	2
Hunt	2	0-0	0-1	2	0	0	0
Marquis	2	0-0	0-0	0	0	0	0
Gelfenbien	1	0-0	0-0	0	0	0	0
Totals	200	25-50	34-46	50	21	13	87

Three-point goals: 3-9, 33.3 (Lobo 2-3, Rizzotti 1-4, Elliott, 0-1, Webber 0-1). **FG pct.:** 50.0; **FT pct.:** 73.9. **Team rebounds:** 8. **TO:** 20. **Blocks:** 5 (Lobo 2, Wolters 2). **Steals:** 10 (Lobo 3). **Fouled out:** Sales.

Halftime — UConn, 44-20
Officials — Sally Bell, Bob Trammell
Attendance — 18,038 at Target Center, Minneapolis

Game 35
April 2
NCAA championship
UConn 70
Tennessee 64

Tennessee

Player	M	FG	FT	RB	A	PF	T
McCray	31	3-12	1-2	5	4	2	7
Thompson	10	1-1	2-2	3	1	2	4
D.Johnson	33	3-11	3-3	10	0	2	9
Marciniak	30	3-11	1-3	0	5	3	8
Davis	31	5-12	0-1	5	1	4	11
Ward	16	2-5	2-2	2	1	3	6
T.Johnson	21	3-7	1-1	5	1	3	7
M.Johnson	13	2-3	0-0	3	1	2	5
Milligan	10	1-3	2-2	0	2	0	4
Conklin	5	1-1	0-0	1	0	1	3
Totals	200	24-66	12-16	37	16	22	64

Three-point goals: 4-14, 28.6 percent (Marciniak 1-6, Davis 1-4, M. Johnson 1-2, Conklin 1-1, McCray 0-1). **FG pct.:** 36.4; **FT pct.:** 75.0. **Team rebounds:** 3. **TO:** 14. **Blocks:** 1 (T. Johnson). **Steals:** 6 (Marciniak 2, D. Johnson 2, McCray, Davis).

Connecticut

Player	M	FG	FT	RB	A	PF	T
Elliott	39	5-7	3-4	7	3	3	13
Lobo	28	5-10	7-8	8	2	4	17
Wolters	31	4-9	2-4	3	0	4	10
Rizzotti	32	6-8	2-2	3	3	3	15
Webber	17	0-1	0-0	1	2	1	0
Sales	33	4-12	1-4	6	3	3	10
Berube	20	1-6	3-5	3	2	0	5
Totals	200	25-53	18-27	43	15	18	70

Three-point goals: 2-10, 20.0 percent (Sales 1-4, Rizzotti 1-2, Lobo 0-2, Webber 0-1, Berube 0-1). **FG pct.:** 47.2; **FT pct.:** 66.7. **Team rebounds:** 12. **TO:** 16. **Blocks:** 4 (Lobo 2, Wolters 2). **Steals:** 7 (Rizzotti 3, Sales 3, Elliott).

Halftime — Tennessee, 38-32
Officials — Dee Kantner, Larry Sheppard
Attendance — 18,038 at Target Center, Minneapolis.

1994-95
UConn women
(35-0)

Exhibition games

Nov. 10: UConn 61, Athletes in Action 58
Nov. 16: UConn 100, Rossianka 77

Regular season games

Nov. 26: at UConn 107, Morgan St. 27
Nov. 27: at UConn 92, Rhode Island 59
Dec. 4: at UConn 80, Villanova 42
Dec. 7: UConn 77, at Holy Cross 52
Dec. 10: UConn 98, at N.C. State 75
Dec. 23: at UConn 101, Iona 42
Dec. 28: at UConn 99, California 52
Jan. 2: at UConn 100, Pittsburgh 67
Jan. 5: UConn 103, at Georgetown 64
Jan. 7: UConn 98, at St. John's 64
Jan. 11: at UConn 104, Providence 50
Jan. 13: at UConn 80, Seton Hall 36
Jan. 16: at UConn 77, Tennessee 66
Jan. 18: UConn 79, at Boston College 54
Jan. 22: at UConn 89, Syracuse 58
Jan. 24: UConn 92, at Miami 51
Jan. 28: UConn 97, at Kansas 87
Jan. 31: UConn 89, at Providence 56
Feb. 5: at UConn 94, Georgetown 72
Feb. 9: at UConn 85, Miami 48
Feb. 12: UConn 84, at Seton Hall 62
Feb. 16: UConn 71, at Pittsburgh 43
Feb. 19: at UConn 86, Boston College 34
Feb. 22: at UConn 103, St. John's 56
Feb. 25: UConn 89, at Syracuse 62
Feb. 27: UConn 79, at Villanova 54

Big East tournament

(Seton Hall, South Orange, N.J.)
March 4: UConn 92, Providence 63
March 5: UConn 95, Pittsburgh 63
March 6: UConn 85, Seton Hall 49

NCAA Tournament

East Regional (Gampel Pavilion, Storrs)
March 16: at UConn 105, Maine 75
March 18: at UConn 91, Virginia Tech 45
March 23: at UConn 87, Alabama 56
March 25: at UConn 67, Virginia 63

Final Four

(Target Center, Minneapolis)
April 1: UConn 87, Stanford 60
April 2: UConn 70, Tennessee 64

Associated Press
Top 25 final
women's poll

First-place votes in parentheses, records through March 13 (does not include NCAA Tournament), points, previous rank:

	Record	Pts	Pv
1. Connecticut (32)	29-0	800	1
2. Colorado	27-2	746	3
3. Tennessee	29-2	742	2
4. Stanford	26-2	695	5
5. Texas Tech	30-3	647	6
6. Vanderbilt	26-6	644	8
7. Penn State	25-4	584	7
8. Louisiana Tech	26-4	583	4
9. Western Kentucky	26-3	557	11
10. Virginia	24-4	522	9
11. North Carolina	28-4	504	10
12. Georgia	24-4	443	12
13. Alabama	20-8	391	13
14. Washington	23-8	364	14
15. Arkansas	22-6	317	15
16. Purdue	21-7	306	16
17. Florida	23-8	281	17
18. George Washington	24-5	276	18
19. Mississippi	21-7	193	19
20. Duke	21-8	186	21
21. Oregon State	20-7	158	24
22. San Diego State	24-5	116	20
23. Kansas	20-10	95	22
24. N.C. State	19-9	58	25
25. Old Dominion	27-5	27	–

Others receiving votes:

Florida International	19
Utah	18
Oklahoma	17
Southern Cal	17
San Francisco	16
Oregon	15
Drake	10
DePaul	9
Southern Miss	9
SMU	7
Wisconsin	7
Memphis State	6
Ohio State	6
Seton Hall	4
Toledo	3
Utah State	2

Final UConn statistics
Record: 35-0

Player	G	Field goals Made -Att.	Pct.	3-point goals Made -Att.	Pct.	Free throws Made -Att.	Pct.	Rebounds Off	Tot	Avg.	Asst	TO	Blk	Stls	Min. -Avg.	Pts.	Avg.
Rebecca Lobo	35	238 -476	50.0	18 -51	35.3	104 -154	67.5	105	343	9.8	129	91	122	40	1005 -28.7	598	17.1
Kara Wolters	33	222 -354	62.7	0 -0	00.0	59 -89	66.3	68	204	6.2	38	60	94	13	761 -23.1	503	15.2
Jennifer Rizzotti	35	156 -308	50.6	57 -138	41.3	69 -94	73.4	19	97	2.8	161	86	2	98	905 -25.9	438	12.5
Nykesha Sales	35	159 -294	54.1	35 -81	43.2	45 -77	58.4	58	162	4.6	73	61	11	102	753 -21.5	398	11.4
Jamelle Elliott	35	131 -253	51.8	14 -24	58.3	106 -129	82.2	101	282	8.1	98	82	3	30	911 -26.0	382	10.9
Carla Berube	33	101 -220	45.9	10 -32	31.3	69 -102	67.6	54	157	4.8	63	60	4	27	626 -19.0	281	8.5
Kim Better	33	47 -112	42.0	5 -23	21.7	59 -92	64.1	28	94	2.8	48	51	1	34	470 -14.2	158	4.8
Pam Webber	35	49 -118	41.5	27 -76	35.5	36 -52	69.2	20	90	2.6	144	65	2	20	847 -24.2	161	4.6
Brenda Marquis	30	35 -60	58.3	0 -0	00.0	8 -14	57.1	16	37	1.2	3	9	3	5	154 -5.1	78	2.6
Kelley Hunt	30	22 -58	37.9	0 -0	00.0	23 -43	53.5	21	55	1.8	11	33	4	8	188 -6.3	67	2.2
Missy Rose	31	20 -64	31.3	7 -22	31.8	11 -18	61.1	8	32	1.0	17	31	2	15	285 -9.2	58	1.9
Jill Gelfenbien	28	4 -17	23.5	0 -0	00.0	2 -2	100	6	22	0.8	1	7	2	0	95 -3.4	10	0.4
UConn	35	1184 -2334	50.7	173 -447	38.7	591 -866	68.2	504	1776	50.7	786	636	250	392		3132	89.5
Opponents	35	762 -2418	31.5	149 -554	26.9	298 -452	65.9	554	1290	36.9	391	742	90	260		1971	56.3

Team rebounds: UConn 201
Deadball rebounds: UConn 100; opponents 69

UConn record book: Player

Career

POINTS
1. 2,177 **Kerry Bascom** 120g (87-91)
2. 2,133 **Rebecca Lobo** 126g (91-95)

REBOUNDS
1. 1,268 **Rebecca Lobo** 126g (91-95)
2. 937 **Peggy Walsh** 108g (82-86)

BLOCKS
1. 396 **Rebecca Lobo**, 126g (91-95)
2. 169 **Kara Wolters**, 66g (93-pres)
3. 162 **Peggy Walsh**, 108g (82-86)

ASSISTS
1. 546 **Pam Webber** 131g (91-95)
2. 541 **Jill Brumbaugh** 107g (85-88)

GAMES PLAYED
1. 131 **Pam Webber** (91-95)
2. 127 **Wendy Davis** (88-92)

FIELD GOAL PERCENTAGE
1. 63.6 **Kara Wolters** (93-pres) 390-618
2. 55.5 **Kathy Ferrier** (89-93) 303-546

Season

REBOUNDS
1. 371 **Rebecca Lobo** 33g (93-94)
2. 343 **Lobo** 35g (94-95)
3. 337 **Peggy Walsh** 27g (85-86)
4. 326 **Lobo** 29g (92-93)

ASSISTS
1. 165 **Jill Brumbaugh** 28g (87-88)
2. 161 **Jennifer Rizzotti** 35g (94-95)
3. 160 **Laura Lishness** 34g (90-91)
4. 153 **Lishness** 31g (89-90)

BLOCKS
1. 131 **Rebecca Lobo** 31g (93-94)
2. 122 **Lobo** 35g (94-95)
3. 97 **Lobo** 33g (92-93)
4. 94 **Kara Wolters** 33g (94-95)

STEALS
1. 102 **Nykesha Sales** 35g (94-95)
2. 98 **Jennifer Rizzotti** 35g (94-95)
3. 86 **Debbie Baer** 34g (91-92)

UConn record book: Team

Season

Most victories (35)
Longest winning streak (35)
Most points (3,132)
Most rebounds (1,776)
Most blocks (250)
Most field goals made (1,184)
Lowest field goal percentage defense (.315)
Highest scoring average (89.5)
Lowest opponent scoring average (56.3)

Game

Most points
(107 vs. Morgan State, 11-26-94)
Largest margin of victory (80 vs. Morgan State)
Highest 3-point field goal percentage
(81.8, 9-11, vs. N.C. State, 12-10-94)
Most 3-point field goals made
(12 vs. Kansas, 1-28-95)
Most blocks
(17 vs. Seton Hall, 1-13-95)

Awards won this season

Geno Auriemma

- **National Coach of the Year:**
  (U.S. Basketball Writers Association; Naismith; Associated Press)
- **Big East Coach of the Year**

Rebecca Lobo

- **National Player of the Year**
  (Naismith; Associated Press; U.S. Basketball Writers Association; Women's Basketball Coaches Association)
- **First team All-America**
  (Associated Press; U.S. Basketball Writers Association; Kodak, Women's Basketball Coaches Association)
- **Kodak All-District I All-America**
- **Big East Player of the Year**
- **Big East first team**
- **Final Four Most Outstanding Player**
- **Final Four All-Tournament team**
- **East Regional All-Tournament team**
- **Big East All-Tournament team**

Jennifer Rizzotti

- **First team All-America** (Kodak)
- **Second team All-America** (Associated Press)
- **Kodak All-District I All-America**
- **Big East first team**
- **Final Four All-Tournament team**
- **East Regional Most Outstanding Player**
- **East Regional All-Tournament team**

Kara Wolters

- **Third team All-America** (Associated Press)
- **Kodak All-District I All-America**
- **Big East second team**
- **Final Four All-Tournament team**
- **East Regional All-Tournament team**
- **Big East tournament Most Outstanding Player**
- **Big East All-Tournament team**

Jamelle Elliott

- **Big East second team**
- **Final Four All-Tournament team**

Nykesha Sales

- **Big East Freshman of the Year**
- **Big East All-Tournament team**

1994-95 UConn team

Players

Kim Better
No. 5
5-7, junior, guard
Suitland, Md.

Missy Rose
No. 10
5-9, sophomore, guard
Scranton, Pa.

Jennifer Rizzotti
No. 21
5-5, junior, guard
New Fairfield

Brenda Marquis
No. 25
6-3, freshman, forward
Moosup

Carla Berube
No. 31
6-0, sophomore, forward
Oxford, Mass.

Pam Webber
No. 32
5-6, senior, guard
Hollidaysburg, Pa.

Jamelle Elliott
No. 33
6-0, junior, forward
Washington

Kelley Hunt
No. 34
6-2, freshman, forward
Londonderry, N.H.

Jill Gelfenbien
No. 40
5-11, senior, forward
Wethersfield

Nykesha Sales
No. 42
6-0, freshman, forward
Bloomfield

Rebecca Lobo
No. 50
6-4, senior, forward
Southwick, Mass.

Kara Wolters
No. 52
6-7, sophomore, center
Holliston, Mass.

Coaching staff

Geno Auriemma
Coach

Chris Dailey
Associate head coach

Meghan Pattyson
Assistant coach

Tonya Cardoza
Assistant coach

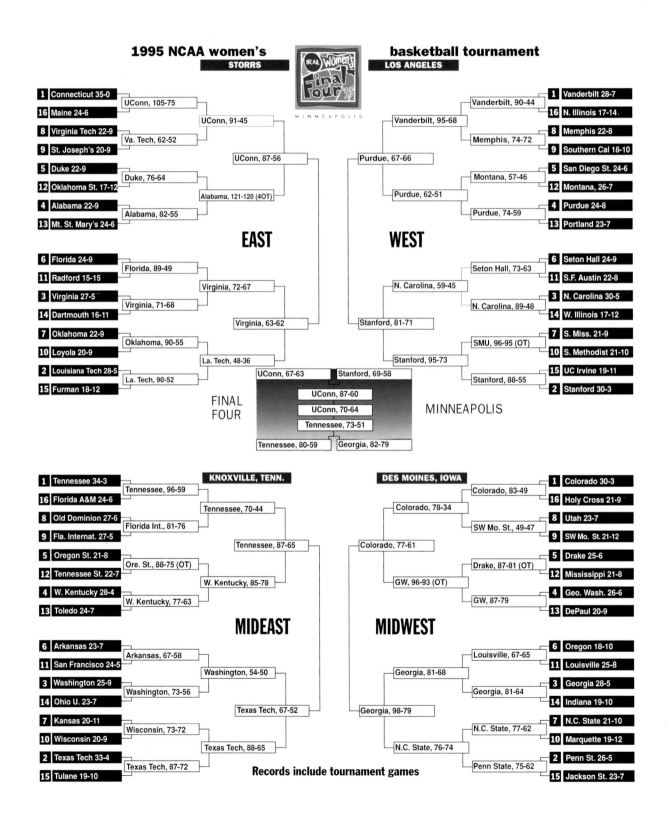

1995 NCAA women's basketball tournament

STORRS

LOS ANGELES

MINNEAPOLIS

EAST

1 Connecticut 35-0	UConn, 105-75
16 Maine 24-6	
8 Virginia Tech 22-9	Va. Tech, 62-52
9 St. Joseph's 20-9	

UConn, 91-45

UConn, 87-56

5 Duke 22-9	Duke, 76-64
12 Oklahoma St. 17-12	
4 Alabama 22-9	Alabama, 82-55
13 Mt. St. Mary's 24-6	

Alabama, 121-120 (4OT)

6 Florida 24-9	Florida, 89-49
11 Radford 15-15	
3 Virginia 27-5	Virginia, 71-68
14 Dartmouth 16-11	

Virginia, 72-67

Virginia, 63-62

7 Oklahoma 22-9	Oklahoma, 90-55
10 Loyola 20-9	
2 Louisiana Tech 28-5	La. Tech, 90-52
15 Furman 18-12	

La. Tech, 48-36

WEST

1 Vanderbilt 28-7	Vanderbilt, 90-44
16 N. Illinois 17-14	
8 Memphis 22-8	Memphis, 74-72
9 Southern Cal 18-10	

Vanderbilt, 95-68

Purdue, 67-66

5 San Diego St. 24-6	Montana, 57-46
12 Montana 26-7	
4 Purdue 24-8	Purdue, 74-59
13 Portland 23-7	

Purdue, 62-51

6 Seton Hall 24-9	Seton Hall, 73-63
11 S.F. Austin 22-8	
3 N. Carolina 30-5	N. Carolina, 89-48
14 W. Illinois 17-12	

N. Carolina, 59-45

Stanford, 81-71

7 S. Miss. 21-9	SMU, 96-95 (OT)
10 S. Methodist 21-10	
15 UC Irvine 19-11	Stanford, 88-55
2 Stanford 30-3	

Stanford, 95-73

FINAL FOUR

UConn, 67-63	Stanford, 69-58

UConn, 87-60

UConn, 70-64

Tennessee, 73-51

Tennessee, 80-59	Georgia, 82-79

MINNEAPOLIS

KNOXVILLE, TENN.

MIDEAST

1 Tennessee 34-3	Tennessee, 96-59
16 Florida A&M 24-6	
8 Old Dominion 27-6	Florida Int., 81-76
9 Fla. Internat. 27-5	

Tennessee, 70-44

Tennessee, 87-65

5 Oregon St. 21-8	Ore. St., 88-75 (OT)
12 Tennessee St. 22-7	
4 W. Kentucky 28-4	W. Kentucky, 77-63
13 Toledo 24-7	

W. Kentucky, 85-78

6 Arkansas 23-7	Arkansas, 67-58
11 San Francisco 24-5	
3 Washington 25-9	Washington, 73-56
14 Ohio U. 23-7	

Washington, 54-50

Texas Tech, 67-52

7 Kansas 20-11	Wisconsin, 73-72
10 Wisconsin 20-9	
2 Texas Tech 33-4	Texas Tech, 87-72
15 Tulane 19-10	

Texas Tech, 88-65

DES MOINES, IOWA

MIDWEST

1 Colorado 30-3	Colorado, 83-49
16 Holy Cross 21-9	
8 Utah 23-7	SW Mo. St., 49-47
9 SW Mo. St. 21-12	

Colorado, 78-34

Colorado, 77-61

5 Drake 25-6	Drake, 87-81 (OT)
12 Mississippi 21-8	
4 Geo. Wash. 26-6	GW, 87-79
13 DePaul 20-9	

GW, 96-93 (OT)

6 Oregon 18-10	Louisville, 67-65
11 Louisville 25-8	
3 Georgia 28-5	Georgia, 81-64
14 Indiana 19-10	

Georgia, 81-68

Georgia, 98-79

7 N.C. State 21-10	N.C. State, 77-62
10 Marquette 19-12	
2 Penn St. 26-5	Penn State, 75-62
15 Jackson St. 23-7	

N.C. State, 76-74

Records include tournament games